FEDERAL TAX POLICIES AND RURAL HOUSEHOLDS

IMPACT AND POTENTIAL REFORM

FEDERAL TAX POLICIES AND RURAL HOUSEHOLDS

IMPACT AND POTENTIAL REFORM

KATHLEEN B. FISHER
EDITOR

New York

For permission to use material from this book please contact us:
Telephone 631-231-7269; Fax 631-231-8175
Web Site: http://www.novapublishers.com

NOTICE TO THE READER

The Publisher has taken reasonable care in the preparation of this book, but makes no expressed or implied warranty of any kind and assumes no responsibility for any errors or omissions. No liability is assumed for incidental or consequential damages in connection with or arising out of information contained in this book. The Publisher shall not be liable for any special, consequential, or exemplary damages resulting, in whole or in part, from the readers' use of, or reliance upon, this material. Any parts of this book based on government reports are so indicated and copyright is claimed for those parts to the extent applicable to compilations of such works.

Independent verification should be sought for any data, advice or recommendations contained in this book. In addition, no responsibility is assumed by the publisher for any injury and/or damage to persons or property arising from any methods, products, instructions, ideas or otherwise contained in this publication.

This publication is designed to provide accurate and authoritative information with regard to the subject matter covered herein. It is sold with the clear understanding that the Publisher is not engaged in rendering legal or any other professional services. If legal or any other expert assistance is required, the services of a competent person should be sought. FROM A DECLARATION OF PARTICIPANTS JOINTLY ADOPTED BY A COMMITTEE OF THE AMERICAN BAR ASSOCIATION AND A COMMITTEE OF PUBLISHERS.

Additional color graphics may be available in the e-book version of this book.

LIBRARY OF CONGRESS CATALOGING-IN-PUBLICATION DATA

ISBN: 978-1-62618-629-3

Published by Nova Science Publishers, Inc. † New York

CONTENTS

PREFACE

The Federal income tax structure has changed substantially over the last two decades. Tax rates have been reduced and deductions and credits, especially refundable tax credits, have expanded, reducing Federal income tax burdens and significantly increasing after-tax income. While these tax reforms have provided the greatest benefit to those with the highest tax liabilities, low- and middle-income rural residents, especially those with children, have been major beneficiaries of some of the changes. This book examines the effect on rural Americans of tax credits targeting low- and middle-income households by estimating the number of beneficiaries, the level of benefits, and the impact of the benefits on income and rural poverty. The relative importance of these tax credits compared with traditional income support programs is also discussed.

Chapter 1 – The authors analyze the increasing use of refundable tax credits targeted to low- and moderate-income households in the Federal individual income tax and determine their implications for rural America. To identify rural and urban households, the analysis matches a zip code approximation of the 2006 Rural-Urban Commuting Area Codes with Internal Revenue Service Individual Income Tax zip code and related data.

These data are then used to examine the impact of the recent expansions to income tax credit programs on affected households. The analysis finds that expansions to both the refundable and nonrefundable portions of the Earned Income and Child Tax credits have provided a major source of income support for low-income workers and their families.

This is especially true in the South, where the rural poor are concentrated.

Chapter 2 - Several proposals calling for fundamental reform of the Federal income tax system have been put forth, including a report by the co-chairs of the National Commission on Fiscal Responsibility. The primary elements of reform—eliminating tax preferences, restructuring capital gains and dividend tax rates, lowering rates on individual income, and reducing the number of tax brackets—could have a significant impact on the after-tax income and well-being of both farm businesses and rural households. This report uses published and special tabulation data obtained from the Internal Revenue Service, farm-level data from USDA's Agricultural Resource Management Survey, and data from the American Housing Survey to examine the current tax situation for farm households and to evaluate the importance of various Federal income tax policies. For farm households, the effect of reform will primarily depend upon changes to existing treatment of investment and business income, including several important business deductions. In contrast, changes to existing individual tax credits, especially refundable tax credits, will likely be of greater significance to nonfarm rural households.

In: Federal Tax Policies and Rural Households   ISBN: 978-1-62618-629-3
Editor: Kathleen B. Fisher   © 2013 Nova Science Publishers, Inc.

Chapter 1

FEDERAL TAX POLICIES AND LOW-INCOME RURAL HOUSEHOLDS[*]

Ron Durst and Tracey Farrigan

ABSTRACT

The authors analyze the increasing use of refundable tax credits targeted to low- and moderate-income households in the Federal individual income tax and determine their implications for rural America. To identify rural and urban households, the analysis matches a zip code approximation of the 2006 Rural-Urban Commuting Area Codes with Internal Revenue Service Individual Income Tax zip code and related data.

These data are then used to examine the impact of the recent expansions to income tax credit programs on affected households. The analysis finds that expansions to both the refundable and nonrefundable portions of the Earned Income and Child Tax credits have provided a major source of income support for low-income workers and their families.

This is especially true in the South, where the rural poor are concentrated.

---

[*] This is an edited, reformatted and augmented version of United States Department of Agriculture, Economic Research Service, Economic Information Bullentin Number 76, dated May 2011.

SUMMARY

What Is the Issue?

Tax credits provided to low- and moderate-income households have grown over the last several decades and now provide a significant boost to the after-tax incomes of taxpayers receiving these credits. This growth has primarily involved enactment of new income tax credits and the expansion of existing ones, especially refundable tax credits (which allow a rebate to the taxpayer of any balance after the credit is applied against the tax owed to the IRS). Two refundable tax credits in particular—the Earned Income Tax Credit (EITC) and the Child Tax Credit (CTC)—have reduced rural poverty and boosted income for low- and middle-income rural households. These and other tax policies, however, could be affected by tax reform or be allowed to expire, since some provisions are only temporary. This report examines the effects of current tax provisions targeting low- and moderate-income households in rural America—focusing on the EITC and the CTC—and compares them with traditional income support programs.

What Did the Study Find?

- Over the last two decades, income tax credits targeted to low-income households have markedly increased. In 1990, the EITC provided $4.4 billion in payments to low-income households; in 2008, the total amount provided by the EITC and the CTC exceeded $64.7 billion.
- In 2008, rural taxpayers reported an average adjusted gross income (AGI) of $43,616 compared with $60,841 for urban taxpayers. The poverty rate was also significantly higher in rural areas (15.1 percent) than in urban areas (12.9 percent).
- Overall, in 2008, one of every three rural taxpayers received benefits from either the EITC or the CTC. These two refundable tax credit programs provided a total of $20.6 billion to rural taxpayers. Of this, $13.7 billion (about two-thirds of the total benefit) exceeded individual taxpayer liabilities and was refunded. These two tax credits provided a 13-percent increase in income, on average, to those receiving one or both of the credits.
- A larger share of eligible households receive the EITC compared with other Federal low-income support program payments, and EITC and

other tax-based benefits represent an increasing share of low-income support funding. However, compared with traditional income-support programs, a greater share of the EITC benefits go to low-income households that are above the poverty level.

How Was the Study Conducted?

This report uses both published and special tabulation data obtained from the Internal Revenue Service (IRS) to evaluate the growth of the EITC, CTC, and other tax credits supporting a variety of social policy objectives. The effect of these policies on rural taxpayers' income and on rural poverty was determined by using a zip code approximation of the 2006 Rural-Urban Commuting Area Codes (to identify rural taxpayers) and matching the zip code data with IRS tax data.

INTRODUCTION

The Federal income tax structure has changed substantially over the last two decades. Tax rates have been reduced and deductions and credits, especially refundable tax credits, have expanded, reducing Federal income tax burdens and significantly increasing after-tax income. While these tax reforms have provided the greatest benefit to those with the highest tax liabilities, low- and middle-income rural residents, especially those with children, have been major beneficiaries of some of the changes.

In recent years, the Federal tax code has become an important vehicle for promoting social policy objectives such as encouraging employment and savings and providing support to families with children. The primary method of providing support has been to allow tax credits, especially refundable tax credits. These include the Earned Income Tax Credit (EITC), the Child Tax Credit (CTC), and the new Making Work Pay Credit. Participation in these tax-based programs is higher than for traditional income support programs, and the tax programs represent an increasing share of total support to low-income households. Thus, the Federal income tax system has played an increasingly important role in Federal support to low- and middle-income taxpayers, especially families with children. Compared with traditional programs such as Temporary Assistance to Needy Families (TANF) or Supplemental Nutrition Assistance Program (SNAP), a larger share of the benefit of the tax credit programs goes to those with incomes above the poverty level. Nevertheless, these tax credits represent a large share of disposable income for many low-income rural families and have reduced the rural poverty rate.

A number of tax provisions enacted or expanded as part of the Economic Growth and Tax Relief Reconciliation Act of 2001 and the American Recovery and Reinvestment Act of 2009 were temporary. Furthermore, interest in tax reform and simplification continues to grow, and the expanding Federal budget deficit is placing increased pressure on policymakers to rein in both direct spending programs and tax expenditures.

This report examines the effect on rural Americans of tax credits targeting low- and moderate-income households by estimating the number of beneficiaries, the level of benefits, and the impact of the benefits on income and rural poverty. (See box, "About the Data.")

The relative importance of these tax credits compared with traditional income support programs is also discussed.

About the Data

Two definitions of rural residence are used in this report: The 2006 Rural-Urban Commuting Area Codes (RUCAs, of the WWAMI Rural Health Research Center) and nonmetropolitan (nonmetro). Nonmetro refers to counties that are outside core-based statistical areas, as identified by the Office of Management and Budget (OMB 2003). RUCAs are a sub-county classification system that utilizes standard Census Bureau Urbanized Area and Urban Cluster definitions, in combination with work-commuting information, to determine rural and urban status and relationships. RUCAs are used as the basis for eligibility for several Federal programs.

Unless otherwise noted, in this report rural residence of taxpayers is based on zip code approximations of the 2006 RUCAs. Corresponding data are from special tabulations of the 2008 Internal Revenue Service Individual Tax Model File and the Brookings Institution Earned Income Tax Credit Series (1997-2007).

The term "taxpayer" is comparable to the Census Bureau definition of a household. It may include a single person as well as a single person or married couple with children.

INCREASED USE OF TAX CODE FOR SOCIAL POLICY GOALS

The Federal tax system has always served purposes beyond the collection of revenue to fund Government programs. However, the system has increasingly been used as a means of promoting or achieving various Government social policy objectives (Berube, 2005). Through various deductions, exclusions, and credits, the tax system is used to encourage home ownership, employment, education, and savings, as well as to provide support for families with children.

Income tax provisions that reduce tax liabilities for targeted activities are often referred to as tax expenditures. Tax expenditures are tax revenue losses attributable to provisions of Federal tax law that allow an exclusion, exemption, or deduction from gross income or which provide a credit, preferential tax rate, or a deferral of tax liability. These expenditures can be considered comparable to direct spending programs, as the two are often used as alternative means of accomplishing social or other policy objectives.

Since 1980, the total cost of tax expenditures has increased by over 250 percent and currently exceeds $1.1 trillion (The White House, 2010). A primary reason for this growth is that there is greater bipartisan support to enact tax expenditures than to fund or increase direct spending programs, especially since tax expenditures are often viewed as tax cuts. These expenditures have significantly reduced the share of taxpayers who owe Federal income tax.

For taxpayers with children, the income tax threshold (with the EITC and CTC) increased from at or below the poverty level in 1985 to more than twice the poverty level by 2005 (fig. 1). (The threshold increase for single taxpayers and married taxpayers without children has not been as dramatic.) As a result, in 2009, only about half of rural taxpayers owed any Federal income tax. This is slightly below the overall rate of 53 percent of all taxpayers and reflects the lower income levels of rural taxpayers.

Taxpayers with no Federal income tax liability cannot benefit from a deduction or nonrefundable credit. This has led to the increased use of refundable tax credits, primarily the EITC and CTC, which often lead to cash payments to taxpayers that owe no Federal income tax. In many instances the amount of the credit also exceeds the amount of the payroll tax. In 2008, 22 percent of rural taxpayers received a cash payment from one or more of the refundable tax credits. The average amount was $2,428. Thus, an effect of the increased use of the tax code for social policy goals has been an increase in the number of rural taxpayers who owe no Federal income tax and who receive a cash payment as a result of the refundable tax credits.

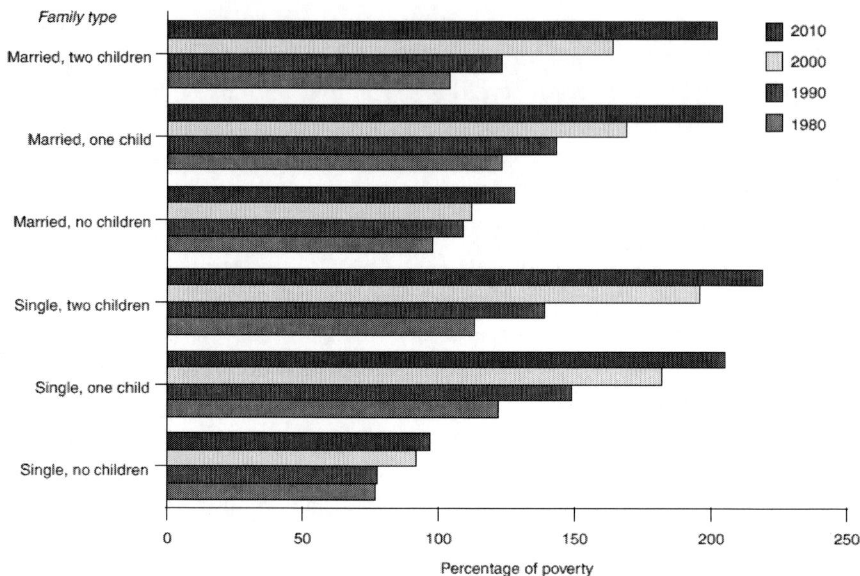

[1]The Child Tax Credit was first effective in 1998, so it is only included in 2000 and 2010.

Source: Economic Research Service using information from the Internal Revenue Service and The Hatcher Group.

Figure 1. Income tax entry threshold with Earned Income Tax Credit and Child Tax Credit[1] as a percentage of poverty level.

SIGNIFICANT FEDERAL TAX POLICY DEVELOPMENTS

While the tax code has historically been used for more than the collection of revenue, the most significant developments in use of the code for social policy objectives have occurred over the last two decades. These developments include both the enactment of several new tax credits and the expansion of existing tax credits, especially the EITC and CTC. These credits, combined with reductions in marginal tax rates, reduced tax rates on dividends and capital gains, marriage penalty relief, and other tax reduction provisions, have provided a significant increase in after-tax income to both rural and urban households. An overview follows of the most important tax expenditures for low- and moderate-income households.

Earned Income Tax Credit

The earned income tax credit (EITC) was enacted in 1975 to reduce the burden of Social Security taxes on low-income workers and to encourage them to seek employment rather than welfare benefits. The original credit was equal to 10 percent of the first $4,000 of earnings and thus could not exceed $400 per year. The Omnibus Budget Reconciliation Act of 1990 expanded the basic credit and provided a larger credit for families with two or more children. The Omnibus Budget Reconciliation Act of 1993 expanded the credit again and added a small credit for childless workers. As a result of the 1990 and 1993 program expansions, the EITC is now one of the largest Federal income-support programs targeted to low-income individuals (Scholz et al., 2009). For 2008, a maximum credit of $4,826 was available to married couples with two or more children. A married couple with one child was eligible for a maximum credit of $2,917, and a childless couple was eligible for a maximum of $438. In 2008, the credit provided an estimated $51.5 billion to nearly 25 million low-income workers and their families, for an average of $2,063 per recipient (fig. 2). Rural residents are major beneficiaries of the expanded credit. While they represent about 18 percent of all taxpayers, they receive about 22 percent of all benefits (fig. 3).

Child Tax Credit

The child tax credit (CTC) is a refundable tax credit for families with children under the age of 17. It was originally enacted as part of the Taxpayer Relief Act of 1997, in response to concerns that the tax code did not fully reflect the ability to pay taxes as family size increased. The credit was originally $500 and refundable only for families with three or more children. The credit was phased out for single taxpayers with incomes in excess of $75,000 and for married couples with incomes in excess of $110,000. The Economic Growth and Tax Relief Act of 2001 increased the credit to $600. The Jobs Growth and Tax Relief Reconciliation Act of 2003 increased the credit to $1,000 and expanded refundability to families with fewer than three children.

In 2008, the CTC provided a total benefit of $51 billion, with $20.4 billion of that amount refunded to taxpayers.

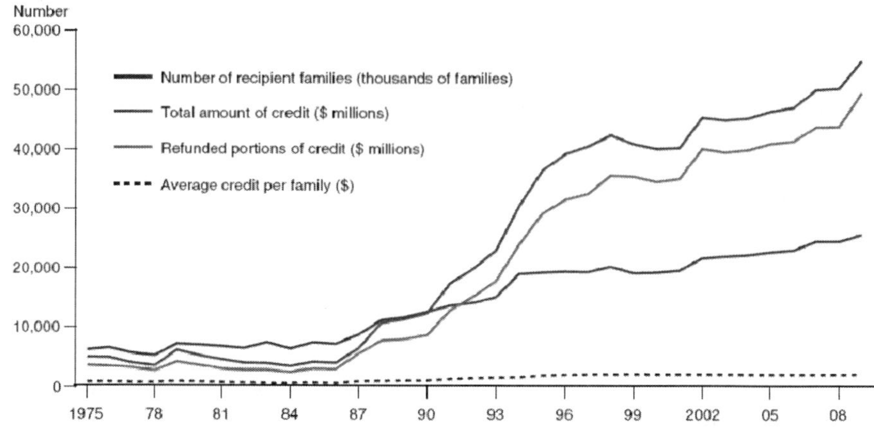

Source: Economic Research Service using data from the internal Revenue Service.

Figure 2. Number of Earned Income Tax Credit recipient families, total amount of credit, and refunded portions of total, 1975-2009.[1]

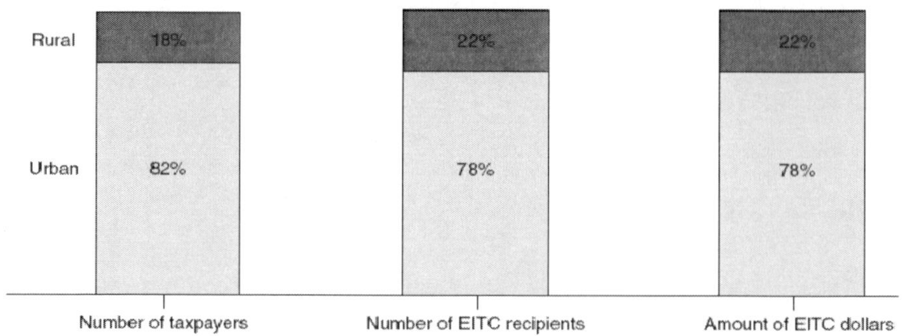

Source: Economic Research Service using data from the Internal Revenue Service.

Figure 3. Distribution of Earned Income Tax Credit (EITC) for rural and urban households, 2008.

Child and Dependent Care Credit

This tax credit, a version of the child care credit, has existed since 1976. The amount of the credit depends upon the income of the taxpayer and the amount of child care expenses. The 2001 Act increased the percentage of eligible expenses allowed and expanded the expenses covered by the credit for 2003 and later tax years. In general, the current credit ranges from 20 to 35 percent, for up to $3,000 of expenses per child or $6,000 total for two or more children. Since the credit is not refundable, moderate-income taxpayers receive more benefits than lower income taxpayers. In 2008, the child and dependent care credit totaled $3.5 billion.

Education Credits

For 2008, the Federal tax code provided two related credits for post-secondary education costs: the Hope Credit and the Lifetime Learning Credit were introduced in 1997 to assist taxpayers with education costs for themselves and their children. The Hope Credit provides up to $1,500 for tuition and fees for the first 2 years of post-secondary education expenses for students who are pursuing a degree at least half-time. The Lifetime Learning Credit is more flexible and provides a 20-percent tax credit for up to $10,000 of costs for students enrolled less than half-time and extends beyond the first 2 years of post-secondary education. Neither of the credits is refundable. The two education credits provided $7.6 billion to 7.7 million taxpayers in 2008.

Saver's Credit

The Saver's Credit was enacted as part of the Economic Growth and Tax Relief Reconciliation Act of 2001. The credit provides a Government match for low- and moderate-income taxpayer contributions to individual retirement or employer-sponsored 401(k) plans. The credit is equal to 10, 20, or 50 percent of the contribution, depending on the level of income. The credit is not refundable and is phased out for single taxpayers with an income above $27,750 and married taxpayers filing a joint return with an income above $55,550. (The effectiveness of the credit in increasing retirement savings is reduced due to its nonrefundability and to the relatively low matching percentage for moderate-income households.) In 2008, only single taxpayers with incomes below $16,500 or married couples with incomes below $33,000 were eligible for the 50-percent match. For the remaining taxpayers, the match was 10 or 20 percent. Thus, both the number of taxpayers claiming the credit and the benefit amounts have been relatively small. For 2008, just under 6 million taxpayers received the credit, receiving a total of $977 million.

RURAL AMERICA RECEIVES A RELATIVELY LARGER SHARE OF BENEFITS

Rural households have historically had lower incomes and a higher poverty rate than urban households. In 2008, rural taxpayers reported an average adjusted gross income (AGI) of $43,616, compared with $60,841 for urban taxpayers. A larger share of rural taxpayers had an AGI below $50,000. While there is little difference between the share of urban and rural taxpayers with incomes between $50,000 and $100,000, the share of urban taxpayers with incomes in excess of $100,000 is more than double that for rural taxpayers. This distribution of income is a primary reason that a larger share of rural taxpayers benefit from the EITC and the CTC. The poverty rate has also been significantly higher in rural areas.[1] In 2008, 15.1 percent of the rural population lived in poverty compared with 12.9 percent of the urban population. One reason for the higher rural poverty rate is the preponderance of low-wage jobs in rural areas. Given the income differential and the prevalence of low-wage jobs, it is not surprising that rural taxpayers receive relatively greater benefits from programs targeted at low-income workers, especially from the EITC.

In 2008, 21.6 percent of rural taxpayers received EITC benefits compared with 16.9 percent of urban taxpayers. However, urban taxpayers receive slightly higher benefits—$2,065 on average compared with $2,061 for rural taxpayers. This reflects the fact that the EITC payment increases as the amount of earned income increases before being phased out at higher income levels. Thus, a married couple with two or more children and $25,000 in income would receive a larger benefit than a similar couple with an income of $10,000. With lower average incomes, rural taxpayers receive slightly lower average EITC payments than urban taxpayers. The share of rural taxpayers who receive the refundable portion of the CTC is also slightly higher, at 13.9 percent compared with 12.6 percent for urban taxpayers.

The earned income and child tax credits provided a total benefit of $20.6 billion to rural taxpayers in 2008. Overall, one of every three rural taxpayers received benefits from either the EITC or the CTC. While most rural taxpayers received less than $3,000, 7 percent received between $3,000 and $5,000, and

4 percent—or about 1 million rural taxpayers—received more than $5,000 (fig. 4). Households receiving more than $5,000 received an estimated total of $5.2 billion in either reduced taxes or cash payments.

Of the $20.6 billion in EITC and CTC benefits going to rural taxpayers, $13.7 billion, or about two-thirds of this amount, was refundable. The refundable portion significantly increases the incomes of lower income rural taxpayers. For rural taxpayers with an AGI under $10,000, refundable credits were nearly a third of the AGI (table 1). The average credit was $1,276. For those with incomes between $10,000 and $20,000, EITC/CTC refundable credits were nearly a fourth of the AGI, or $3,474 on average. Overall, these credits provided a 13-percent increase in income to taxpayers receiving one or both of the credits. Also, since tax refunds generally do not constitute income in determining eligibility or benefits under other federally funded income support programs, benefits under traditional support programs are not reduced by refundable credits.

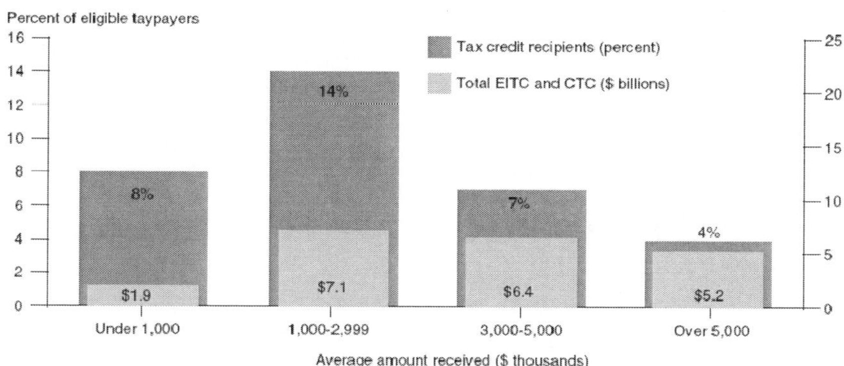

EITC = Earned Income Tax Credit; CTC = Child Tax Credit.
Source: Economic Research Service using data from the Internal Revenue Service.

Figure 4. Share of rural taxpayers and total amount of EITC and CTC received, by average amount, 2008.

Compared with the EITC and the CTC, the child care, education, and saver's credits benefit a relatively small share of rural taxpayers with relatively small amounts. These credits combined provided less than $1.8 billion to rural taxpayers in 2008. A larger share of urban taxpayers received the education and child care credits, while a larger share of rural taxpayers received the saver's credit. Only about 4.4 percent of rural taxpayers received the education credit in 2008, for an average benefit of $981. An even smaller share of rural taxpayers claimed the child care credit, with 3.6 percent of rural taxpayers receiving an average credit of $487. A slightly higher share of rural taxpayers claimed the saver's credit—5.6 percent compared with 3.9 percent for urban taxpayers. However, the average credit amount for rural taxpayers was only $171.

Table 1. Refundable credits and adjusted gross income for rural taxpayers by level of adjusted gross income, 2008

Refundable earned income and child tax credits	Adjusted gross income		Credits as share of adjusted grossincome
Adjusted gross income	*$ Millions*	*$ Millions*	*Percent*
Under $10,000	2,026	6,442	31
$10,001 to $20,000	6,025	25,620	24
$20,001 to $25,000	2,383	16,148	15
$25,001 to $50,000	2,968	45,730	6
$50,001 to $100,000	273	12,472	2
Over $100,000	2	220	1
All	13,680	106,633	13

Source: Economic Research Service, based on special tabulations from 2008 Internal Revenue Service (IRS) tax data.

TAX CREDIT PROGRAMS HAVE GROWN IN IMPORTANCE RELATIVE TO TRADITIONAL INCOME SUPPORT PROGRAMS

The three largest Federal income support programs for low-income households are the EITC, Supplemental Nutrition Assistance Program (SNAP—formerly food stamps), and Temporary Assistance to Needy Families (TANF—formerly Aid to Families with Dependent Children). Prior to 1990, the Federal outlay for the EITC was substantially below that for SNAP and TANF (fig. 5). Expansions to the EITC that occurred in 1990 and that have since continued have resulted in tax code program expenditures now rivaling those of the more traditional welfare expenditure programs. For example, based on the 2012 Federal Budget, the actual EITC outlay for 2008 was slightly larger (by 3.3 percent) than SNAP and significantly larger (by 86.1 percent) than TANF.

However, the Federal budget estimates for 2009 and 2010 show a significant increase in SNAP for low-income households not matched by outlays for the EITC. Outlays for programs such as SNAP and unemployment insurance automatically increase during economic downturns to meet rising needs. Spending levels for those programs have also increased more than in the past due to the policies enacted to combat recessionary impacts. For instance, SNAP, unemployment insurance, and expanded health insurance benefits are the primary income support programs that have impacted the budget through the American Recovery and Reinvestment Act of 2009 (ARRA). While estimated costs of the ARRA expansions of those income support programs are less than the tax-based program expansions, they provide a larger share of total benefits to lower income households (Mattingly, 2009a and b).

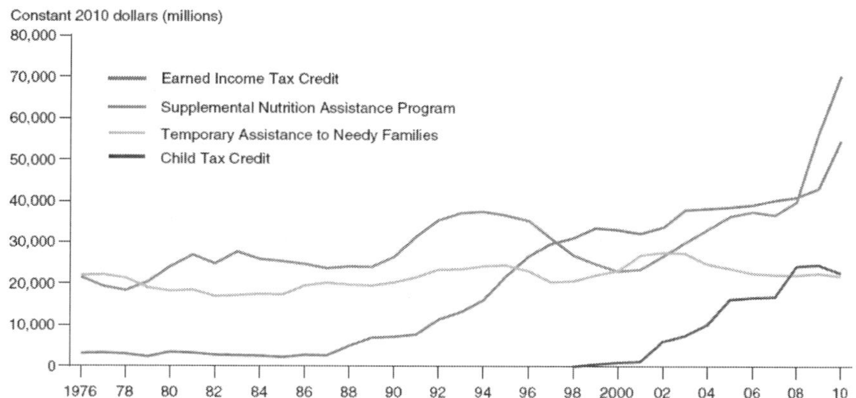

Source: Economic Research Service using data from FY 2012 U.S. Government Budget (U.S.G.P.O.).

Figure 5. Annual Federal outlays for Earned Income Tax Credit, Child Tax Credit, Supplemental Nutrition Assistance Program, and Temporary Assistance to Needy Families.

Aside from annual outlays, there are several features that distinguish the EITC and other tax credits like the CTC from SNAP and TANF. One is the fact that only taxpayers who work are eligible for EITC and the refundable portion of the CTC. Another is that—unlike in-kind (SNAP) and other cash (TANF) benefits—refundable tax credits are entirely administered through the tax system. This has important implications for participation and compliance rates, administrative costs, and the ways in which recipients perceive tax credit incentives.

TAX CREDIT "PARTICIPATION" EXCEEDS THAT OF TRADITIONAL INCOME SUPPORT PROGRAMS

Compared with seeking benefits from other programs designed to provide income support to low-income households, claiming the EITC is relatively easy. Since most eligible households are already required to file an income tax return, all that is necessary is to complete a couple of extra forms and file them with the return. It is not necessary to fill out a separate application or visit an office to establish eligibility for benefits.

As a result, the EITC provision has been especially successful in reaching low-income families with children. Throughout the 1990s, participation by this group ranged from 80 to 86 percent and was 85 percent for families with two or more children in 2005 (Burman and Kobes, 2005). In that year, the overall participation rate was 75 percent. The participation rate was significantly lower for individuals and families without children, reaching only about 55 percent in 2005. One reason for this lower participation rate is the relatively small size of the credit compared with the amount available to families with children.

While a larger share of rural taxpayers claim the EITC than urban taxpayers, there is some evidence that a significant number of eligible taxpayers in rural American are not filing for the credit due to limited availability of information and resources such as free tax preparation sites, which are more prevalent in urban areas. Outreach efforts in several urban areas have increased awareness of the credit and led to increased participation. The Internal Revenue Service has targeted workers in rural areas for outreach efforts to educate eligible taxpayers about the EITC and to encourage them to file for the credit. Those efforts include increasing the availability of volunteer tax preparation services so that taxpayers who need help filing their returns can take advantage of the expansion in EITC and other tax credits. As a result, users of volunteer tax preparation services went from about 1 out of every 75 rural filers receiving the EITC in 2000 to 1 out of every 8 rural filers receiving the EITC in 2007. Studies indicate that users of volunteer services tend to include public assistance recipients, young adults, the elderly, those with low levels of educational attainment, those who lack homeownership, racial/ethnic minorities, and single females with children (Liebman, 1998).

TAX CREDITS FACE TARGETING AND DELIVERY CHALLENGES

While participation rates for tax credit programs may be higher than for traditional income support programs, implementing social policy through the tax code is not without its disadvantages. The EITC has experienced a relatively high error rate in that a large number of EITC recipients received more than they should have or were not eligible for the credit because they did not meet all of the eligibility criteria. The erroneous payment rate is estimated at between 23 and 28 percent (IRS, 2008). Overpayments can be attributed both to unintentional error and to fraud. The Internal Revenue Service has initiated efforts to address this problem through increased customer service, education and outreach, and enhanced enforcement activities. The effort has increased the administrative costs of the program, although they still remain relatively low compared with traditional income support programs.

Another difficulty with tax credits is the timing of payments. Many income support programs provide a benefit at regular intervals on a weekly or monthly basis. Most individuals receive EITC and refundable child tax credit payments as a lump sum when they file their tax return. Research has shown that these lump sum payments are primarily used to repay loans or bills and to improve access to transportation. The once-a-year funds are not available to pay daily living expenses.

A further disadvantage arises because the EITC and refundable portion of the CTC increase as earnings increase before being phased out at higher income levels. With regard to the EITC, this partly reflects the original purpose of the credit—to offset the payroll tax and to encourage work. While this provides increased benefits to those in poverty, it means that households with incomes of less than half the poverty level receive lower benefits than those at or slightly above the poverty level. In 2008, those with incomes below $10,000 received refundable credits of $1,276 on average, while those with incomes between $10,000 and $20,000 received $3,475. Thus, for those earning at or below the income level at which benefits are phased out, a decline in earnings as a result of a job loss or reduced hours could result in a drop in an eligible household's credit payment just as the household's need increases. This is exactly the opposite path of traditional income support programs, which tend to increase support with increased need.

Finally, each of these credits has numerous eligibility criteria to target benefits to intended recipients. These criteria add considerable complexity to an already complex tax code, increasing the administrative burden on both the taxpayer and the Internal Revenue Service.

REFUNDABLE TAX CREDITS HAVE CONTRIBUTED TO REDUCED POVERTY RATES

Refundable tax credits, especially the EITC, have lifted a significant number of households above the poverty line. As noted, for taxpayers with children, the income tax threshold with the EITC and CTC has increased from at or below the poverty level in 1985 to more than twice the poverty level by 2005. In 2005, the EITC lifted an estimated 5.1 million individuals above the poverty level, including 2.6 million children (Sherman, 2009b). This was more than any other single program, including SNAP and the TANF program.

While the official measure of poverty does not include the EITC as a form of income, the Census Bureau publishes information on poverty under various alternative definitions. Comparing the poverty rate under the definition of income for various support programs and the EITC with the official poverty estimates for 2006 suggests a reduction in the rural poverty rate from 15.1 percent to 11.1 percent (U.S. Census Bureau). The EITC alone was responsible for a reduction of 1.7 percentage points in the rural poverty rate. This suggests that in 2006, the EITC lifted an estimated 800,000 rural residents above the poverty line. Given the expansions in the EITC and refundability of the CTC that have occurred since 2006, as well as increases in the number of States that offer EITC benefits supplemental to the Federal benefit, the current impact on rural poverty is likely to be even greater. (See box, "Federal Policies Have Been Supplemented by State Policies.")

The impact of the expanded EITC on the rural poor is indicated in part by the geographic distribution and share of tax return filers receiving the credit. The percentage of rural taxpayers who received the EITC in 2007 was greatest in the South (fig. 6), where a large percentage of the Nation's rural poor has historically resided. The median rate of the EITC receipt for Southern States is 21.2 percent of rural households that filed a tax return.

Federal Policies Have Been Supplemented by State Policies

State earned income tax credits supplement the Federal credit and can contribute to efforts to reduce child poverty, increase effective wages, and cut taxes for low- and moderate-income working families. Since 1986, 24 States and the District of Columbia have enacted an EITC. Nearly one-third were enacted between 2005 and 2010, including the one in the State of Washington, the first among nine States without a broad-based income tax to enact a State EITC.

These credits are generally based on the Federal EITC. Most of the States use Federal eligibility rules and express the State credit as a specified percentage of the Federal credit, which in 2010 ranged from 3.5 percent in Louisiana to 75 percent in Maryland. As with the Federal EITC, refundability is an important feature of most State EITCs. All but two States with an EITC have made the credit at least partially refundable.

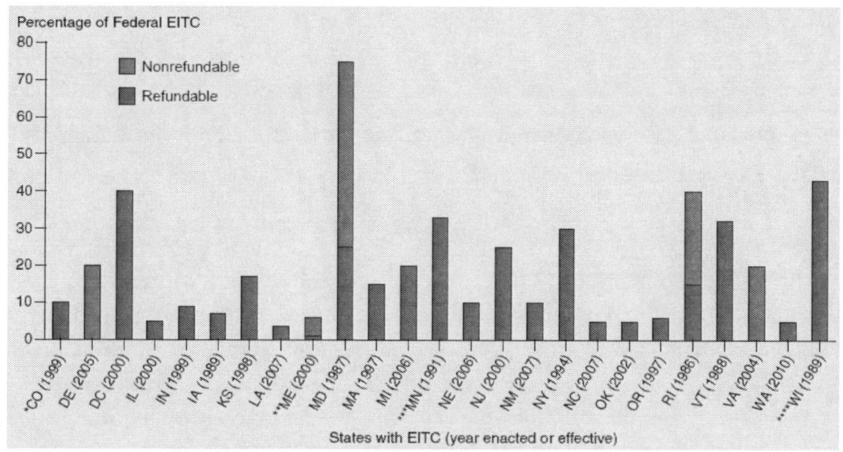

* Suspended since 2001 and will not be reinstated until at least 2013.
** Refundable portion is maximum $150 for joint filers / maximum $125 for single filers.
*** Average-percentage varies by income.
****Maximum-percentage varies by number of children.
Source: Economic Research Service using information from the Internal Revenue Service and The Hatcher Group.

States with Earned Income Tax Credit (EITC), year enacted or effective, percentage of Federal credit, and refundability.

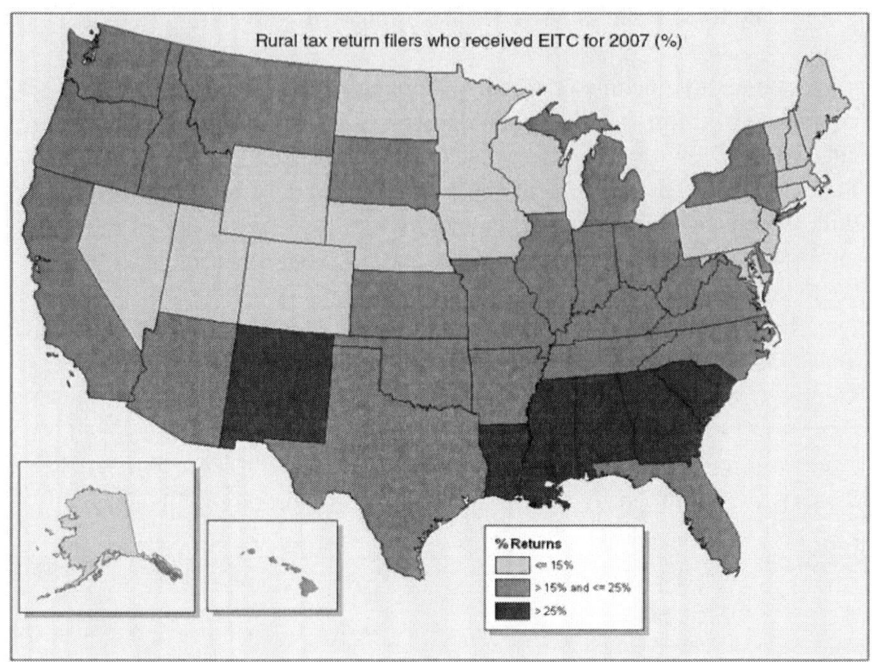

Source: Economic Research Service using data from Brookings Institution EITC
series.

Figure 6. Earned Income Tax Credit (EITC) receipts, percent of filers.

This compares with 13 percent of rural households in Northeastern States
and 15 percent in the Midwest and the West. These differences reflect higher
average income levels in rural areas outside of the South, particularly in the
Northeast.[2]

Accounting for the effects of EITC and other sources of income-related
assistance using an alternative measure of poverty increases mean and median
incomes for vulnerable populations, such as single females with children and
racial and ethnic minorities, but it still leaves many low-income families below
the poverty line. This is a result of the program's focus on the working
population and the fact that an increasing share of the benefit goes to the near-
poor, those with an income level just above their poverty income threshold.
Those most likely to have been raised out of poverty by tax credits and other
income support programs are the poor whose income level is not far below
their poverty income threshold. Families in that category who qualify for EITC
typically include married couples with children, where the likelihood that the
household will contain a full-time worker is greatest. Therefore, reduction of

the marriage penalty and increases in credits available to larger families has benefited that group in particular.

RECENT POLICY CHANGES PROVIDE EXPANDED BENEFITS

The American Recovery and Reinvestment Act of 2009 (ARRA) made a number of changes to temporarily provide an income boost to low-income taxpayers. These changes included expanded benefits for both the EITC and CTC. The act also added a new refundable tax credit, the Making Work Pay Credit, aimed at low- and middle-income workers.

The ARRA made two important changes to the EITC for 2009 and 2010. First, it increased the amount of the credit for families with three or more children. For 2009 and 2010, they were eligible for an additional $629, increasing the maximum credit for such families to $5,666 (fig. 7). The act also reduced the marriage penalty by increasing the income range over which the EITC is phased out for married taxpayers by $5,000. These changes are estimated to boost the EITC for rural taxpayers by more than 10 percent, with much of the additional benefit going to married taxpayers with three or more children.

The ARRA also increased the refundable portion of the CTC. Since the refundable portion of the credit is limited to 15 percent of income over a threshold amount, families with low incomes may not be eligible for the refundable CTC or may receive a reduced amount. The act lowered the income threshold from $8,500 in 2008 to $3,000 for 2009 and 2010. For a family with two children and an income of $10,000, this could increase the refundable credit from $225 to $1,050. This change is estimated to increase the refundable portion of the CTC to rural taxpayers by about one-third.

The ARRA also provided a new refundable credit for 2009 and 2010. The Making Work Pay Credit provided a refundable credit of 6.2 percent of earnings (the employee share of the old-age portion of the Social Security payroll tax), up to $400 for an individual and $800 for a married couple. The credit was phased out at a rate of 2 percent of income over $75,000 for an individual and $150,000 for married couples filing a joint return. About four out of five returns filed by rural taxpayers received the credit. The estimated benefit to rural taxpayers in 2010 was $10.75 billion, with an average benefit of $535.

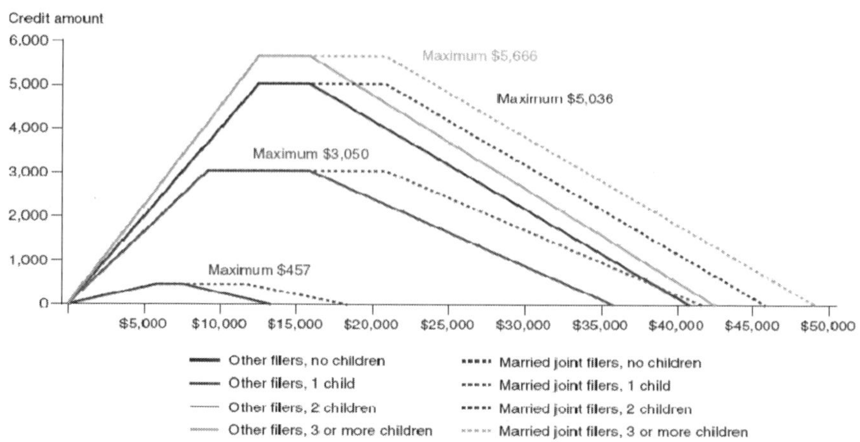

Source: Economic Research Service using data from the Internal Revenue Service.

Figure 7. Value of the Earned Income Tax Credit by income, 2010 Credit amount.

When combined, these credits are expected to soften the impact of the recession by providing additional income support and keeping a significant number of taxpayers from falling below the poverty line. It has been estimated that the expansions of the EITC, CTC, and the new Making Work Pay Credit will prevent 1 million children from falling below the poverty line (Sherman, 2009a). For rural taxpayers, these credits are estimated at nearly $36 billion, with about two-thirds of this amount received as cash payments through the refundable portion of the tax credits. The Tax Relief, Unemployment Reauthorization and Job Creation Act of 2010 extended the EITC and CTC provisions through 2012. While the Making Work Pay Credit expired, a reduction in the Social Security tax rate on employees from 6.2 to 4.2 percent was provided for 2011. A comparable reduction of 2 percentage points was also provided for the self-employment tax rate. While this reduction will provide greater tax relief to rural taxpayers overall, low-income individuals with earned income below $20,000 will receive less in tax relief and refund payments than with the Making Work Pay Credit.

CONCLUSION

The Federal Tax Code has become an increasingly important vehicle for promoting social policy objectives. Not only do these policies reduce Federal income tax burdens and the share of taxpayers who owe taxes, but they also provide income support to low- and middle-income families through refundable tax credits. This is especially true for rural taxpayers, whose income tends to be lower than that of urban taxpayers. As a result, rural taxpayers receive a disproportionately large share of the benefits, especially from the EITC and the CTC.

Many of these policies were enacted or expanded as part of the Economic Growth and Tax Relief Reconciliation Act of 2001, the Economic Growth and Tax Relief Reconciliation Act of 2003, and the American Recovery and Reinvestment Act of 2009 and were scheduled to expire at the end of 2010. The Tax Relief, Unemployment Reauthorization and Job Creation Act of 2010 extended the expansions to the EITC and CTC, as well as other expiring provisions, through the end of 2012. As the increasing Federal budget deficit puts additional pressure on policy officials to rein in direct spending and tax expenditures, and as the push for comprehensive tax reform grows, the effectiveness of these provisions in achieving their policy objectives is certain to be reevaluated. The resulting decisions to modify or extend these expenditures will be of considerable importance to rural America.

GLOSSARY

Rural —Our classification of counties as "rural" for purposes of this analysis includes counties designated as nonmetropolitan (nonmetro) by the Office of Management and Budget in 2006. Nonmetro counties are defined as those counties lying outside urban cores of 50,000 people or more and their immediately adjacent commuting zones. For more detail on how nonmetro areas are defined, and how they differ from the U.S. Census Bureau's definition of rural, see the ERS briefing room, "Measuring Rurality: What is Rural?" http://www.ers.usda.gov/Briefing/Rurality/WhatIsRural/.

Poverty rate—The percentage of households with a federally specified annual income less than the amount deemed sufficient to purchase basic needs of food, shelter, and clothing and other essential goods and services for its members is classified as "poor." The poverty threshold is set by the Office of Management and Budget and varies by household size, constituency and, over time, with the cost-of-living index. In the 2000 Census of Population, information on income was collected for 1999. The threshold for a family of four, including two children, was $16,985. For further information on the definition of poverty see: http://www.census.gov/hhes/www/ poverty/povdef. html.

Refundable tax credit—A refundable tax credit is a credit that is payable in full even if it exceeds the taxpayer's Federal income tax liability. Most tax credits are not refundable and can only be used to offset the taxpayer's tax liability.

REFERENCES

Berube, Alan. 2005. *The Tax Code as Social Policy in Rural America*, RPRC Working Paper No. 05-08. December.

Brookings Institution, Earned Income Tax Credit Series, available at: http://www.brookings.edu.

Burman, Leonard E., and Deborah I. Kobes. *EITC Reaches More Eligible Families Than TANF, Food Stamps*. Tax Notes, March 17, 2003.

Economic Research Service, U.S. Dept. of Agriculture. United States Fact Sheet: Population, Income, Education, Employment, and Federal Funds, http:www.ers.usda.gov/State Facts/US.htm. Accessed May 24, 2010.

Hatcher Group. 50-State Resource Chart, State EITC Online Resource Center, available at: http://www.stateeitc.com.

Internal Revenue Service, U.S. Dept. of Treasury. States and Local Governments With Earned Income Tax Credit, EITC page, available at: http://www.irs.gov.

Internal Revenue Service, U.S. Dept. of the Treasury. IRS Earned Income Tax Credit (EITC) Initiatives: Report on Qualifying Child Residency Certification, Filing Status, and Automated Underreporter Tests, January 2008. http://www.irs.gov/pub/irs-utl/poc_summary_addendum_121708_final.pdf.

Jolliffe, Dean. 2006. *The Cost of Living and the Geographic Distribution of Poverty*. Economic Research Service, U.S. Dept. of Agriculture, Economic Research Report Number 26, September. http://www.ers.usda.gov/Publications/ERR26/ERR26.pdf.

Liebman, Jeffrey B. 1998. "The Impact of the Earned Income Tax Credit on Incentives and Income Distribution," *Tax Policy and the Economy*, Vol. 12.

Mammen, Sheila, and Frances C. Lawrence. *Use of the Earned Income Tax Credit by Rural Working Families*. 2006 Conference of the Eastern Family Economics and Resource Management Association.

Mattingly, Marybeth. 2009a. *Forty-Three Percent of Eligible Rural Families Can Claim a Larger Credit with EITC Expansion*, Fact Sheet No. 12, Carsey Institute, University of New Hampshire.

Mattingly, Marybeth. 2009b. *Seventy-Eight Percent of Working Rural Families To Receive Full Making Work Pay Tax Credit*, Fact Sheet No. 14, Carsey Institute, University of New Hampshire.

Sherman, Arloc. 2009a. *Recovery Agreement Temporarily Expands Child Tax Credit for Large Numbers of Children in Every State.* Center on Budget and Policy Priorities, February 12.

Sherman, Arloc. 2009b. *Safety Net Effective at Fighting Poverty but Has Weakened for the Very Poorest.* Center on Budget and Policy Priorities, July 6.

Scholz, John Karl, Robert Moffitt, and Benjamin Cowan. 2009. "Trends in Income Support," in *Changing Poverty, Changing Policies*, M. Cancian and S. Danziger, editors. Russell Sage Foundation, New York, pp. 203-41. http://www.ssc.wisc.edu/~scholz/Research/ Transfers_Chapter_2008_V6.pdf.

The White House. 2010. The Moment of Truth: Report of the National Commission on Fiscal Responsibility and Reform. December. http:// www.fiscalcommission.gov/sites/fiscalcommission.gov/files/documents/ TheMomentofTruth12_1_2010.pdf.

WWAMI Rural Health Research Center. http://depts.washington.edu /uwrhrc/index.php

U.S. Census Bureau. Current Population Survey (CPS), Annual Social and Economic Supplement, Table RD-REV POV01, available at: http:// pubdb3.census.gov/macro/032007/pov/new01_000.htm.

U.S. Government Printing Office, Historical Budget Tables, Budget page, available at: http://www.gpoaccess.gov.

Williams, E., N. Johnson, and J. Shure. 2009. State Earned Income Tax Credits: 2009 Legislative Update. Center on Budget and Policy Priorities, available at: http://www.cbpp.org.

End Notes

[1] The official poverty measure from the U.S. Census Bureau assumes that the cost of living is the same throughout the United States. The Federal Government is examining experimental poverty measures, however, that adjust poverty rates according to geographic cost-of-living differences (Jolliffe, 2006).

[2] A smaller share of taxpayers in urban areas received the credit in 2007, which is the normal pattern. The median urban rate of taxpayers who receive the credit is 18.6 percent in Southern States, 11.5 percent in the Northeast, 12.9 percent in the Midwest, and 13.1 percent in the West.

In: Federal Tax Policies and Rural Households   ISBN: 978-1-62618-629-3
Editor: Kathleen B. Fisher   © 2013 Nova Science Publishers, Inc.

Chapter 2

THE POTENTIAL IMPACT OF TAX REFORM ON FARM BUSINESSES AND RURAL HOUSEHOLDS[*]

James M. Williamson, Ron Durst and Tracey Farrigan

ABSTRACT

Several proposals calling for fundamental reform of the Federal income tax system have been put forth, including a report by the co-chairs of the National Commission on Fiscal Responsibility. The primary elements of reform—eliminating tax preferences, restructuring capital gains and dividend tax rates, lowering rates on individual income, and reducing the number of tax brackets—could have a significant impact on the after-tax income and well-being of both farm businesses and rural households. This report uses published and special tabulation data obtained from the Internal Revenue Service, farm-level data from USDA's Agricultural Resource Management Survey, and data from the American Housing Survey to examine the current tax situation for farm households and to evaluate the importance of various Federal income tax policies. For farm households, the effect of reform will primarily depend upon changes to existing treatment of investment and business income, including several important business deductions. In contrast, changes to

---

[*] This is an edited, reformatted and augmented version of United States Department of Agriculture, Economic Information Bulletin, Publication No. 107, dated February 2013.

existing individual tax credits, especially refundable tax credits, will likely be of greater significance to nonfarm rural households.

SUMMARY

What Is the Issue?

Proposals calling for fundamental tax reform have once again called attention to a tax system that many regard as overly complex, inefficient, and inequitable. Proponents of reform see this as an opportune time for a comprehensive overhaul of the tax system because major features of the system are set to change, although some were recently made permanent by the American Taxpayer Relief Act of 2012.

Several proposals calling for fundamental reform of the Federal income tax system have been put forth, including a report by the co-chairs of the National Commission on Fiscal Responsibility (NCFRR), a bipartisan reform panel created by the President in 2010 to address the fiscal stability of the United States. The primary elements of proposed reform—eliminating tax preferences, restructuring capital gains and dividend tax rates, lowering rates on ordinary income, and reducing the number of tax brackets—could have a significant impact on the after-tax income and well-being of both farm businesses and rural households.

What Did the Study Find?

The primary goals of tax reform are to simplify the tax system, making compliance easier and reducing economic distortions induced by the system, while preserving its progressive nature. While reform may improve societal welfare, the current tax system contains features that provide substantial benefit to *farm businesses* in the form of reduced rates on capital gains, accelerated cost recovery provisions, and other special deductions for farm production activities. Since most farms are operated as sole proprietors, partnerships, or other noncorporate entities and taxed under the individual income tax, reform of the individual income tax structure is of greatest importance to most farmers. However, reform of the corporate income tax could also affect important business tax provisions for farmers, including those taxable under the individual income tax.

In particular, reducing or eliminating deductions for capital purchases and raising capital gains taxes could increase the farmer's tax base and raise the tax rate paid on a significant portion of their income. These effects will vary by farm size. Offsetting these effects, though, is the proposed reform of the marginal tax rate structure. A reduced number of brackets and lower rates could mitigate the effect of a potentially larger tax base for many U.S. farm households.

In 2010, about 38 percent of U.S. farmers, defined as taxpayers who filed a Schedule F with their Form 1040, reported some *capital gains*—nearly three times the share for all other taxpayers—totaling $28.4 billion. The average amount of capital gain reported by farmers was also more than double the average capital gain reported by other taxpayers. If capital gains are taxed at rates equal to income tax rates, farmers will face higher tax liabilities on capital gains income, even if ordinary tax rates are reduced.

Farming requires large investments in machinery, equipment, and other depreciable capital. In 2010, U.S. farmers reported a total of $29 billion on capital purchases, and those making investments made an average of $32,000 in annual capital purchases. Proposed restrictions on current *expensing and accelerated recovery of capital purchases* could increase taxable income, especially during the early years following tax reform. Under present law, the maximum expensing amount is $500,000, but will drop to $25,000 in 2014 (as provided by the American Taxpayer Relief Act of 2012). While fewer than 20 percent of small farms (those with less than $250,000 of gross sales) invest more than $25,000, nearly 54 percent of commercial farms (farms with at least $250,000 of gross sales) invest more than that amount. Thus, investment by commercial farms will be affected the most by a substantially lower expensing amount. This could lead to increased taxable income and reduced capital investment by these farms.

Commercial farms are also the primary beneficiaries of the domestic production activities deduction for manufacturers. While only about 7 percent of farms claimed the deduction, the total amount deducted was $1.25 billion. For these farms, eliminating the deduction could add an average of about $9,000 to their taxable income.

About one out of seven farmers uses the *self-employed health insurance deduction* in any given year. In 2010, these farmers deducted an average of $6,173 for a total of $1.684 billion in health insurance premiums. Over 50 percent of farm households obtain their insurance through off-farm employment of the operator or spouse, which helps account for the low number of farmers claiming the deduction. Many other farmers are over age

65 and are covered by Medicare or other Government programs. Nonetheless, tax reform that eliminates the deduction for premiums on health insurance purchased by the self-employed could increase taxable income for some farmers.

Tax reform would affect rural nonfarm households differently than farm and urban households. Rural taxpayers are likely to have lower incomes and be older than urban households. Given their lower income, *rural nonfarm households are less likely to benefit from tax deductions*, exemptions, exclusions, or deferrals, because they either lack eligible expenses to exceed the standard deduction or otherwise do not qualify for the tax exemption. Some of the most widely used deductions—for mortgage interest and real estate taxes—are related to the value of property and real property tax rates, which are generally lower in rural areas. Although rural households have higher rates of home ownership, they are less likely to have a mortgage. Thus, the typical rural homeowner may even benefit if the current mortgage interest deduction was replaced with a refundable credit for mortgage interest because the credit does not require taxpayers to itemize to receive the benefit or even have a tax liability at all.

While rural households would be less affected than other households by the elimination of itemized deductions, the restructuring of *refundable tax credits* could significantly lower the after-tax income of low-income rural households. Any reform that reduces the value of refundable credits—especially the Earned Income Tax Credit (EITC) and Child Tax Credit (CTC)—is likely to reduce the well-being of low-income rural households. Overall, one out of every three rural taxpayers receives benefits from the EITC or the CTC. In 2008, 21.6 percent of rural taxpayers received EITC benefits, compared with 16.9 percent of urban taxpayers. The earned income and child tax credits provided a total benefit of $20.6 billion to rural taxpayers in 2008.

How Was the Study Conducted?

This report uses both published and special tabulation data obtained from the Internal Revenue Service to provide an overview of the current tax situation for U.S. farm households and to evaluate the importance of various Federal income tax policies. It also uses farm-level data from USDA's Agricultural Resource Management Survey to estimate the effects of various policies on Federal income tax liabilities of farmers. The American Housing

Survey is also analyzed to evaluate the relative importance of various tax provisions for rural households.

INTRODUCTION

Tax reform has once again become a topic of discussion among policymakers and the general public. Proposals calling for fundamental reform of the Federal income tax system have raised awareness of features of the system that many regard as overly complex, inefficient, or inequitable. Proponents of reform argue that the system, with its patchwork of tax preferences, is needlessly complicated and expensive to administer. Proponents also see this as an opportune time for a comprehensive overhaul of the tax system because major features of the system are set to change, although some features were recently made permanent by the American Taxpayer Relief Act of 2012.

Legislation enacted in the Economic Growth and Tax Relief Reconciliation Act of 2001 (EGTRRA) and the Jobs and Growth Tax Relief Reconciliation Act of 2003 (JGTRRA) expired at the end of 2012. However, the American Taxpayer Relief Act of 2012 made permanent or extended many of the provisions in those acts important to farm businesses and rural households.[1] Under current law, the marginal tax rates on ordinary income under $400,000 ($450,000 for couples) remain at the current rates, as does the rate on capital gains and dividends; certain preferential accelerated capital cost recovery provisions also remain.

This report examines recommendations put forth in a report by the co-chairs of the National Commission on Fiscal Responsibility and Reform (NCFRR) for addressing the Federal tax system. The Commission was a bipartisan reform panel created by the President in February 2010 to address the fiscal stability of the United States. This report represents common reform themes expressed by stakeholders and policymakers that will likely serve as a blueprint for future tax reform.[2] The elements of reform discussed in this report—eliminating or restructuring tax preferences such as mortgage interest deductions, restructuring capital gains and dividend tax rates, lowering marginal tax rates, and reducing the number of tax brackets—could have a significant impact on the after-tax income and well-being of farm businesses and rural households. We use tax return data from the Internal Revenue Service (IRS), income and balance sheet data from USDA's 2010 Agricultural Resource Management Survey (ARMS), and house ownership and mortgage data from the American Housing Survey to examine the size and scope of farm business and rural household activities that currently benefit from provisions identified as targets for reform (For additional information on data sources and definitions, see box).

Data Sources and Definitions

Internal Revenue Service Income Tax Data

The Internal Revenue Service annually collects and publishes information on the operation of the Internal Revenue laws. This report uses both published and special tabulation data obtained directly from the Internal Revenue Service to evaluate the effect of various tax policies on farmers and rural America by level of adjusted gross income. *Adjusted gross income* is income from all sources, including net farm income/loss, minus certain adjustments to income.

For tax purposes, a *farm* is defined as a taxpayer who has farm income or expense and files a schedule F Federal income tax return. http://www.irs.gov/uac/Tax-Stats-2

Agricultural Resource Management Survey Data

The annual Agricultural Resource Management Survey (ARMS) is USDA's primary source of information on the financial condition, production practices, and resource use of America's farm businesses and the economic well-being of America's farm households.

The report uses income and balance sheet information from the survey to evaluate various policies and to differentiate the impact by farm size based on gross sales. For purposes of the survey, a *farm* is defined as any place from which $1,000 or more of agricultural products were produced and sold, or normally would have been sold, during the year. http://www.ers.usda.gov   /data-products/arms-farm-financial-and-crop-production-practices.aspx

American Housing Survey Data

The American Housing Survey is the most comprehensive national housing survey in the United States. It provides current information on a wide range of housing subjects.

The survey is used in this report to obtain information on home ownership and mortgage amounts. http://www. census.gov/housing/ahs/

OBJECTIVES OF FUNDAMENTAL TAX REFORM

The impetus to reform the tax system is the nearly universal desire to make the tax system simpler to administer and comply with, to improve its efficiency, and to ensure equitable treatment. To accomplish such goals, reform proponents often refer to "broadening the tax base," or amending the Internal Revenue Code (IRC) to include more income as taxable by eliminating tax expenditures or preferences.[3] Tax expenditures, the top ten by expense shown in table 1, are defined as Federal revenue losses attributable to special tax exclusions, exemptions, and deductions, as well as preferential tax rates, credits, and deferrals of tax liability (OMB, 2012). Broadening the tax base by eliminating tax expenditures can reduce complexity and computational burden, and perhaps increase efficiency and equity.

Table 1. Top ten individual tax expenditures, 2011

Expenditures	Estimates ($ billion)
Exclusion of employer contributions for health care, health insurance premiums, and long-term care insurance premiums	109.3
Reduced tax rates on dividends and long-term capital gains	90.5
Deduction for mortgage interest on owner-occupied residences	77.6
Earned Income Tax Credit	59.5
Child Tax Credit	56.4
Exclusion of pension contribution and earnings to defined contribution plans	48.4
Exclusion of pension contribution and earnings to defined benefit plans	42.7
Deduction of non-business State and local government income taxes, sales taxes, and personal property taxes	42.4
Exclusion of capital gains at death	38.0
Exclusion of untaxed social security and railroad retirement benefits	31.0
Exclusion of untaxed benefits provided under cafeteria plans[*]	31.0
Total	626.8

*A "cafeteria plan" is a type of employer-provided benefit plan that allows employees to receive certain benefits—for example, accident and health benefits, adoption assistance, or dependent care assistance—on a pretax basis, .

Source: Joint Committee on Taxation, January 2012, Estimates of Federal Tax Expenditures for Fiscal Years 2011-2015, JCS-1-12, table 1.

Maintaining the progressive nature of the current tax system is also a stated goal of reform. Generally, progressivity is measured as a function of taxes paid relative to income. If the average tax rate increases with income, the system is said to be progressive. Progressivity can also be measured by the system's impact on the change in the relative after-tax income shares across the population of taxpaying households. A progressive system will reduce the after-tax income of taxpayers relative to their pre-tax incomes as taxpayers' incomes increase.

Simplifying the Tax System

Complying with the tax code can be time consuming and costly if help with preparation is needed. More than three out of five U.S. taxpayers paid for tax preparation in 2006 (GAO, 2007). The need for assistance is not limited to taxpayers who would traditionally have complex tax filings, like individuals who receive income through partnerships or other pass-through entities, including a majority of farmers. Many tax credits are targeted to low-income families with children, and on average, a family receives multiple credits. Further, each credit may require a complex series of calculations, carried out through multiple forms, and guided by different eligibility rules. Filers may not be aware of the tax benefits available to them because of the labyrinth of rules, and accessing the benefits may require paying for preparation assistance. This complexity may also result in taxpayers' failure to report income or file appropriately, and in some cases failure to file altogether. The IRS estimated the tax gap—the difference between taxes owed and taxes paid— was $345 billion in 2001 (GAO, 2011).

Improving Efficiency

Taxes affect decisions about resource allocation, including the decision to participate in an activity and the level of effort of the activity for those who participate. The labor force participation decision is often cited as an example. Tax rates influence a person's decision to participate in the labor force, as well as how many hours to work, by altering the after-tax rate of pay. Proponents also suggest that the tax preferences in the current system distort such economic decisions by changing relative prices of economic activities. From the perspective of societal well-being, preferential tax treatment can cause distortions to arise when relative price differentials encourage taxpayers to consume, save, and invest differently than they would without such distortions. By removing preferential tax treatment, many of the tax-induced economic distortions can be lessened or eliminated.

Many proponents of tax reform argue that current tax rates—seven brackets ranging from a rate of 10 to 39.6 percent—are too high and discourage work and investment, leading to inefficiency. On the other hand, higher tax rates may encourage more work if taxpayers choose to maintain their current standard of living rather than trade consumption for leisure. Further, the preferential treatment of gains from capital income may encourage an inefficient allocation of resources to unearned income; in particular, higher income individuals have the ability to substitute their remuneration between ordinary income and capital income. However, the extent to which a taxpayer's labor-supply decisions are influenced by the after-tax value of earnings is an empirical question.[4] Further, many of the provisions in the IRC, such as the Earned Income Tax Credit (EITC) and Child Tax Credit (CTC), are subject to phaseout once a taxpayer's income reaches a certain level. When the graduated tax brackets combine with the credit phaseout rates, taxpayers face even greater effective tax rates, which could lead some to work less in order to avoid the phaseout.[5]

Equity Concerns

The Federal tax system has been criticized for violating the concepts of vertical and horizontal equity. Simplifying the tax code by eliminating deductions may address some equity concerns. The principle of vertical equity requires that taxpayers across the income distribution are taxed in proportion to their ability to pay, and proponents of reform note that the system of deductions violates this principle because higher income individuals benefit more from deductions due to their higher marginal tax rates. From the standpoint of vertical equity, credits offer an advantage over itemized deductions because the tax value of each dollar of credit is equal for all taxpayers, no matter the taxpayer's marginal tax rate.

On the other hand, in many cases, the system treats similarly situated taxpayers differently—or treats taxpayers with the same income differently—violating the principle of horizontal equity. The different tax treatment of earnings and capital gains is a notable example. Under current law, a taxpayer with $50,000 of earned income from salaries, wages, or business endeavors will face a significantly higher tax burden than a taxpayer whose income consists of $50,000 of unearned income from dividends or capital gains.

REFORM PROPOSALS

The bipartisan National Commission on Fiscal Responsibility and Reform was created in February 2010 by the President to "[identify] policies to improve the fiscal situation in the medium term and to achieve fiscal sustainability over the long run."[6] The Commission's co-chairs released a report in December 2010 entitled "The Moment of Truth," offering multiple variations of tax reform scenarios that rely on eliminating itemized deductions and restructuring or creating new credits, as well as lowering the statutory marginal rates.

Itemized deductions are targeted for reform because they add complexity to the tax system and reduce equity and progressivity. Proponents of reform argue that itemized deductions complicate the Federal tax system and create differences in tax liability between taxpayers with similar incomes and filing status—a violation of the principle of horizontal equity. Further, itemized deductions reduce the progressivity of the tax system because their value depends on the taxpayer's marginal tax rate, generally reducing tax liability more for a high-income taxpayer than for a low-income taxpayer. Thus, the impact of reducing or eliminating itemized deductions would be more keenly felt by high-income taxpayers. This is true, for example, with respect to the mortgage interest deduction, which is typically one of the largest itemized deductions for most taxpayers.

To start, the Commission's proposal would eliminate all special tax preferences and use revenue from the savings to lower tax rates and add back "small and more targeted" provisions that accomplish policy goals, such as promoting the labor force participation of low-income households, home-ownership, health, charity, and retirement saving. Under the co-chairs' illustrative plan, the widely used deduction for mortgage interest would be replaced with a 12-percent nonrefundable credit applied to the annual interest on a mortgage worth no more than $500,000 in original value.[7]

The deduction for charitable donations would also be eliminated and replaced with a 12-percent nonrefundable credit with a 2-percent adjusted gross income (AGI) floor—that is, the credit would only apply to donations to the extent that they exceed 2 percent of a taxpayer's AGI.

The NCFRR co-chairs' plan would simplify retirement saving by consolidating retirement accounts and limit the aggregate annual amount that could be contributed to the lesser of $20,000 or 20 percent of income.

Under current law, the interest income received from State and municipal bonds is not taxable and has been treated as such for nearly a century. The co-chairs' proposal would tax the interest income on all newly issued State and municipal bonds, including "Aggie Bonds" issued by States, which provide loans to beginning farmers with low equity.

The co-chairs' plan also calls for a limit or "cap" on the tax treatment of employer-sponsored health care insurance. Under current law, 100 percent of the cost of an employer's contribution for health insurance is excluded from taxation, and this represents the largest tax expenditure in terms of cost—over $109 billion a year (see table 1)—covering close to 150 million individuals in America (Kaiser Foundation, 2011).

The proposal calls for the exclusion to be reduced to the 75th percentile of premium values in 2014 and kept at this level through 2018, effectively reducing the value of the exclusion, though only for beneficiaries whose plans exceed the imposed cap. By 2038, however, the proposal would completely phase out the exclusion, and tax the full extent of employers' contribution to health insurance.

The NCFRR report also proposes to reduce the statutory marginal tax rates and condense them to three brackets—the lowest rate could be as low as 8 percent and the maximum rate no higher than 29 percent.[8] Capital gains and dividends would be taxed at these new lower ordinary rates.

Two other notable tax reform plans have also been released recently (see appendix table A1). In August 2010, The President's Economic Recovery Advisory Board—an advisory panel tasked by the President with assembling options to reform the tax system—released a report with options to simplify the IRC for individual taxpayers, increase taxpayer compliance, and reform the corporate tax system.

The Bipartisan Policy Center also issued a proposal by their Debt Reduction Task Force[9] entitled "Restoring America's Future." Both of these proposals share common features with the NCFRR co-chairs' report, such as lowering marginal rates on ordinary income, equalizing capital gains and ordinary income tax rates, reducing tax expenditures, reducing itemized deductions, consolidating credits, and streamlining the tax-filing process. The Bipartisan Policy Center plan proposes a national sales tax as well.

TAXATION OF FARM INCOME UNDER PROPOSED REFORM

The Federal income tax is a progressive tax imposed on net income. It is collected annually and accounts for a substantial portion of total Federal tax revenues. Reform of the Federal income tax could have a significant effect on investment, management, and production decisions in the agricultural sector.

The individual income tax is significantly more important than the corporate income tax for understanding how taxes affect most farmers. Sole proprietorships, partnerships, and subchapter S corporations are all taxed at the individual level. The most common form of farm organization is the sole proprietorship which, according to the 2007 Census of Agriculture (USDA, National Agricultural Statistics Service), accounted for 86.5 percent of all farms and 50 percent of total sales. Partnerships comprise 7.9 percent of farms and 20 percent of sales. Income from farm partnerships and corporations taxed under subchapter S of the IRC (known as S Corporations) is also passed through to the individual partners or shareholders for taxation at the individual shareholder or partner level. Corporate farms, including C-corporations and S-corporations, in total represent 4.4 percent of U.S. farms and account for about 30 percent of sales. While census data do not separate S-corporations from other corporations, family-held corporations account for about 90 percent of all corporations, and many of these family-held corporations are S-corporations. The remaining 1.3 percent of farms includes cooperatives, estates, trusts, and institutional farms. Some of the income from these farms is also taxed under the individual tax rate structure. Therefore, more than 96 percent of all farms and over 75 percent of farm sales are taxed under the provisions of the individual income tax.

Although most family income and a large share of farm income is taxed under the individual tax structure, this does not mean that reform of the corporate tax structure would have no impact on agriculture.[10] The NCFRR co-chairs recommended replacing the graduated corporate tax rate structure with one rate; they suggested a 28-percent tax rate, depending upon the number of corporate tax expenditures that are eliminated. Since most farm corporations are relatively small, with income taxed at less than the top rate, eliminating the graduated rate structure could shift the tax burden from larger to smaller corporations.[11] For instance, the current tax rate on the first $50,000 of taxable income is 15 percent. Thus, smaller farm corporations could not only lose deductions as tax expenditures are eliminated but face higher tax rates on their expanded income tax base if the current rate structure is replaced with a single rate.

Corporate tax reform could also affect capital cost recovery and the domestic production activities deduction. Changes to these business tax provisions as part of corporate tax reform could also have a significant impact on the farm business income and tax liability of sole proprietors, partners, and other farm businesses taxed under the individual tax structure.

Most Federal Income Tax for Farm Households Is Paid on Off-Farm Income

Farm households receive income from both farm and off-farm activities, and for many, off-farm income accounts for a large share of the household's total income. In 2011, the average farm household income reported in the ARMS survey was $87,289, and off-farm sources accounted for a majority of the income (84.3 percent). In fact, since 1980, farm sole proprietors as a group have reported negative aggregate net farm income for tax purposes, and over the last decade, both the share of farmers reporting losses and the amount of losses reported have increased (fig. 1). About half of all farm partnerships and small business corporations also report losses.

In 2010, based on IRS data, nearly three of every four farm sole proprietors reported a farm loss. For those who reported a loss, the average loss was $18,079 for a total of $24 billion. This increased reporting of losses has coincided with an increase in the amount of capital investment that can be expensed in the first year; that and other tax law changes may partially explain the trend of increasing reported farm losses.

Because the family is the typical unit of taxation for a farm business, farm and nonfarm income are combined when computing Federal income taxes for farm households. Most Federal income tax paid by farm households can be attributed to nonfarm income. With only about 30 percent of farm sole proprietors reporting a profit and with just 60 percent of those reporting a farm profit owing any Federal income taxes, only about 19 percent of farm sole proprietors paid any Federal income tax on their schedule F farm income in 2010.

Table 2 provides information on average income, farm profit/loss, and taxes by level of adjusted gross income for farm sole proprietors in 2010. While farm sole proprietors reported average adjusted gross income and taxes of $85,021 and $12,664, respectively, they also reported a net farm loss of $6,064, on average. Because taxes on farm income are paid at the individual level, under the proposed changes to the individual income tax system, farm households could experience significant changes to their after-tax incomes. Proposed changes to the system of deductions and credits will expand the taxpayer's tax base, and proposed changes to tax rates on dividends and capital gains, in particular, will raise current tax rates for some farmers, even if the plan is designed to be revenue neutral.

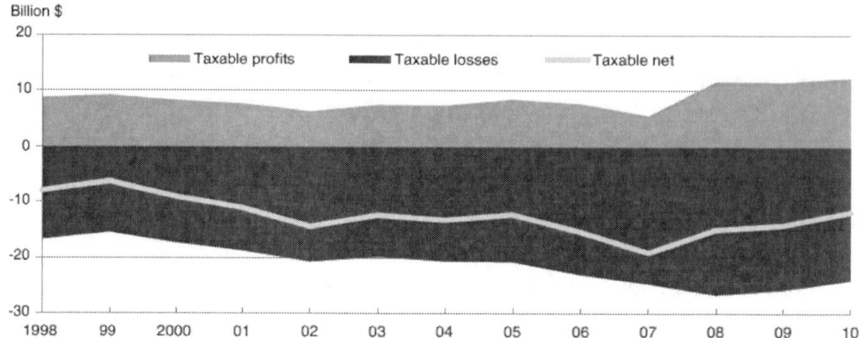

Source: USDA, Economic Research Service; tax data are compiled from the Internal Revenue Service.

Figure 1. Total taxable net farm income/loss for farm sole proprietors reported on Form 1040 Schedule F, 1998-2010.

Table 2. Average farm profit/loss, income tax liability, and tax rate for farm sole proprietors by level of adjusted gross income, 2010

Level of adjusted gross income	Number of returns	Average adjusted gross income	Average farm profit/loss	Average Federal income tax	Average effective income tax rate
		Dollars	*Dollars*	*Dollars*	*Percent*
No adjusted gross income	152,600	(115,827)	(27,746)	106	-
$1 to $10,000	155,440	5,051	(5,092)	8	.2
$10,001 to $25,000	242,271	17,285	(6,457)	116	.7
$25,001 to $50,000	413,386	37,148	(5,025)	1,067	2.9
$50,001 to $100,000	554,953	72,088	(3,181)	4,858	6.7
$100,001 to $250,000	339,874	141,398	(800)	17,376	12.3
Over $250,000	76,206	944,714	(13,488)	203,773	21.6
All	1,934,731	85,021	(6,064)	12,664	15.1

Source: USDA, Economic Research Service, based on special tabulations from 2010 Internal Revenue Service (IRS) tax data.

Farmers Realize a Greater Share of Their Income from Capital Gains Than the Average Taxpayer

Reform would likely alter the tax treatment of capital gains. The Federal income tax system has historically taxed gains on the sale of assets held for investment purposes at lower rates than on other sources of income. The current tax rate on capital gains is 15 percent for taxpayers below the 39.6-percent income tax bracket and 20 percent for those in the 39.6-percent bracket (0 percent for taxpayers in the 10- or 15-percent income tax brackets; in addition, certain high-income taxpayers are assessed a 3.8 percent surtax). These reduced rates are especially significant for farmers because some assets used in farming or ranching are eligible for capital gains treatment and the amount of capital gains is increased by the ability to currently deduct certain costs (e.g., maintenance or depreciation). A primary source of such gains (or losses) is the sale of cattle used for breeding, dairy, draft, or sporting purposes; and certain other livestock.[12] Under current tax law, the IRC allows for proceeds from the disposition of such business property to be treated as a capital gain (or loss).

Under the reform proposals, the preferential tax rate for capital gains would be eliminated and replaced with a rate that is equal to the rate on ordinary income. According to the IRS, in 2010 about 38 percent of all farmers reported some capital gains—more than three times the share for all other taxpayers. The average amount of capital gain reported by farmers was also more double the average capital gain reported by other taxpayers. In 2010, the last year for which complete IRS data are available, farmers reported capital gains of $28.4 billion.[13] This amount represented about 21.5 percent of total taxable income reported by farm households. The average amount for those reporting capital gains or losses was $38,921.

A large amount of this capital gain income was reported by high-income farmers with adjusted gross income over $250,000. Capital gains accounted for one-third of the taxable income for this group. Although high-income farmers comprised less than 4 percent of sole proprietorships filing returns, they accounted for 74.2 percent of all capital gains reported by farmers and reported average capital gains of $362,200 (table 3). On average, nearly one-third of reported gains by farm sole proprietors are attributed to the sale of assets used in farming.

The share of farms reporting capital gains income also increases with farm size. Over 60 percent of commercial farmers reported capital gains income, accounting for 25 percent of all capital gains reported by farmers. However, most of the capital gain is from the sale of nonfarm assets, especially for residential/lifestyle farmers (Durst and Monke, 2001).[14]

Table 3. Share of returns and average capital gain and income from the sale of business assets for farm sole proprietors by level of adjusted gross income, 2010

Level of adjusted gross income	Total number of returns	Share reporting capital gain/loss	Average capital gain	Share reporting sale of business assets	Average gain on business assets	Business asset share of total capital gain
		Percent	Dollars	Percent	Dollars	Percent
No adjusted gross income	152,600	47.0	21,090	28.8	10,952	31.8
$1 to $10,000	155,440	25.4	3,159	16.0	2,762	55.0
$10,001 to $25,000	242,271	27.0	3,122	16.3	3,881	75.1
$25,001 to $50,000	413,386	33.9	4,476	16.3	6,429	68.9
$50,001 to $100,000	554,953	33.6	13,518	18.7	7,985	46.0
$100,001 to $250,000	339,874	49.4	15,792	17.6	22,434	50.7
Over $250,000	76,206	77.9	362,200	31.9	204,003	23.1
All	1,934,731	37.8	38,921	18.8	22,748	29.1

Source: USDA, Economic Research Service, based on special tabulations from 2010 Internal Revenue Service tax data.

A 2007 IRS *Sales of Capital Assets* study reported that net gains from the sale of livestock were $2.2 billion, while gains from the sale of farmland were $4.6 billion. The data include farmers and nonfarmers who held the assets (many nonfarmers hold investments in agriculture but do not materially participate in farming) and demonstrate the high value that the assets generate upon their sale.

Limits on Accelerated Capital Cost Recovery Could Affect Farmers' Capital Purchase Decisions

Farming requires large investments in machinery, equipment, and other depreciable capital. Under the current tax system, such costs may be treated as a current expense or capitalized and depreciated over time. In either case, this reduces the income subject to tax. The amount that can be expensed is subject to a limit, and the investment amount above the limit must be depreciated over a specified recovery period, generally 7 years for farm machinery and equipment.

Based on 2010 ARMS data, U.S. farmers reported a total of $29 billion in capital purchases, and those making investments made $32,000, on average, in annual capital purchases.

The tax treatment of these investments is of considerable importance to the farm sector, especially to commercial farmers (farm sales above $250,000). Over the last decade, the amount that a farmer could immediately expense has changed. Beginning with the Economic Growth and Taxpayer Relief Reconciliation Act of 2001 (2001 Act), which set the expensing amount at $25,000, the amount of capital purchases eligible for immediate expensing has steadily increased (table 4). The amount was raised from $25,000 to $100,000 in 2003, and then again in 2008 to $250,000 through stimulus legislation. The Small Business Jobs Act of 2010 doubled the expensing amount to $500,000 for property placed in service in 2010 and 2011.[15] The Tax Relief, Unemployment Insurance Reauthorization, and Job Creation Act of 2010 extended the modified expensing amount, but the amount was lowered to $139,000 for property placed in service in tax year 2012. The American Taxpayer Relief Act of 2012 temporarily increases the amount to $500,000 for 2012 and 2013.

The ability to take an additional first-year depreciation deduction also benefits farmers making capital purchases. Combined with the expensing amount, the ability to accelerate depreciation has meant that much of the capital purchases made during the past decade have been completely deducted in the first year (table 4). For tax years 2012 and 2013, the first-year depreciation allowance is 50 percent.

In 2010, 43 percent of U.S. farms made a capital investment, but the percentage varies by farm size. In general, the greater the sales revenue of the operation, the more likely it is to make a capital investment in a given year. Based on 2010 ARMS data, 83 percent of very large commercial farms—farms with at least $500,000 in annual sales—reported they made such an investment in 2010, while only 36 percent of farms classified as rural residences (less than $250,000 in sales and a reported occupation other than farming) made a capital investment.

The impact of tax reform on U.S. agricultural investment will depend on how the expensing and depreciation provisions change. Currently, fewer than 18 percent of farmers annually invest more than the prior 2012 expensing limit of $139,000 while only a little over 1 percent invest more than the revised

2012 and 2013 limit of \$500,000. Investments above this amount are eligible for the 50-percent additional first-year depreciation, so nearly all capital investment by farmers can be written off in the current year. The capital expensing allowance reduces the effective tax rate on income from farm capital and simplifies the recordkeeping burden associated with the depreciation of capital purchases, with commercial farmers the primary beneficiaries.

Table 4. Expensing amount limits and additional first-year depreciation, 2000-2014

Tax year	Expensing amount	Additional first-year depreciation
	Dollars	*Percent*
2000	20,000	0
2001-02	24,000	30
2003	100,000	50
2004	102,000	50
2005	105,000	50
2006	108,000	0
2007	125,000	0
2008	250,000	50
2009	250,000	50
2010	500,000	100[1]
2011	500,000	100
2012	139,000[2]	50
2013	500,000	50
2014	25,000	0

[1]Property acquired and placed in service after September 8, 2010.
[2]Indexed for inflation; Source: Revenue Procedure 2011-52. Retroactively increased to
    \$500,000 by the American Taxpayer Relief Act of 2012.
Source: Internal Revenue Code Sections 165 and 179.

Eliminating or lowering the expensing amount would raise the cost of capital purchases for some farms. Currently, few farms exceed the limits on the expensing provision, and as the amounts decrease, it is the farms with the largest business receipts that are constrained by the expensing amount. Under present law, the maximum expensing amount will become \$25,000 in 2014. While 2010 ARMS data indicate that fewer than 20 percent of residential and intermediate farms (farms with less than \$250,000 of gross sales) invest more than \$25,000, nearly 54 percent of all commercial farms (farms with at least \$250,000 of gross sales) invest more than that amount (fig. 2). Thus, investment by commercial farms will be affected the most by a substantially lower expensing amount. This could lead to increased taxable income and reduced capital investment by these farms.

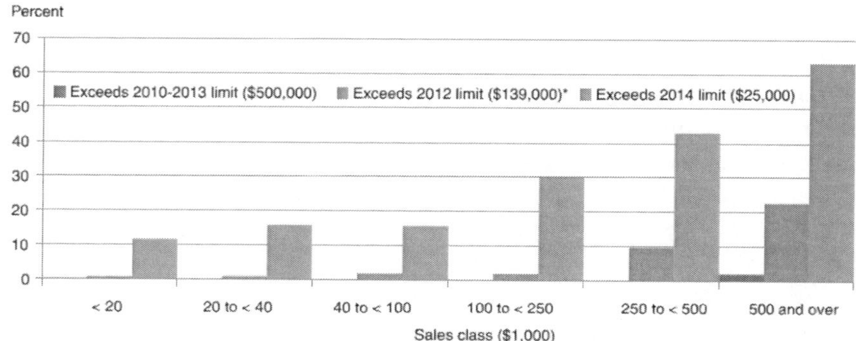

* Retroactively increased to $500,000 by the American Taxpayer Relief Act of 2012.
Source: USDA, Economic Research Service, Agricultural Resource Management Survey, 2010.

Figure 2. Farms with agricultural investments exceeding the expensing limit, by gross farm sales, 2010.

As well as raising the cost of capital investment, lowering or eliminating expensing and additional first-year depreciation could increase the farm's tax base, potentially increasing its taxable income. On average, farmers reported depreciation expenses of $21,259 in 2010. Farms with $500,000 or more of annual sales had an average depreciation expense of $94,000. Farmers that had previously been able to write off most or all of their capital investment in the first year due to the expensing and first-year depreciation provisions will find that their taxable incomes are higher with the scaling back or elimination of these provisions, whether they adjust their investment levels or not, and this could result in higher tax burdens.

Income Averaging

Under a progressive tax rate system, taxpayers whose annual income fluctuates widely may pay higher total taxes over a multiyear period (due to bouncing among tax brackets from year to year) than other taxpayers with similar yet more stable income. Farm business income is more variable than many other sources of income, such as wages and salaries. Mishra et al. (2002) estimate that farm business income accounts for 46.5 percent of the annual variation in farm household total income, while off-farm wages account for 23.2 percent. Farm business income is susceptible to commodity price volatility, which embodies the risks of weather and natural phenomena. As such, variability of farm household income generally exceeds that of all U.S. households.

Variability in farm income across time is attributed to fluctuations in farm output, commodity prices, and business cycles. Farmers are allowed to use various income tax provisions to manage their tax liabilities. Cash accounting, which recognizes income and expenses when received or paid, can reduce taxable income through prepaid business expenses or deferred farm income, and, as discussed above, well-timed capital purchases can reduce taxable income through depreciation deductions or capital expensing. While these provisions are useful in reducing income variability, they are limited by the ability of a farmer to defer sales or accelerate expenditures.

Income averaging can reduce the effect of a progressive tax rate system on taxpayers with variable income by allowing them to smooth their tax burdens over time through tax accounting methods that consider multiyear income. U.S. farmers have been eligible for income averaging since 1998. Under the current income averaging provision, a farmer can elect to shift a specified amount of farm income, including gains on the sale of farm assets other than land, to the preceding 3 years and to pay taxes at the rate applicable to each year. Income that is shifted back is spread equally among the 3 years. If the marginal tax rate was lower during 1 or more of the preceding years, a farmer may pay less tax than he or she would without the option of income averaging. The provision, however, does not allow income from previous years to be brought forward. Furthermore, although the provision is designed to reduce the effect of farm income variability, as long as some farm income is available to be shifted, the source of income variability does not need to be farm income for income averaging to be beneficial.

In 2004, according to IRS tax data, 50,800 farmers—or about 2.5 percent of farms—reduced their tax liability on average by $4,434 with income averaging. The reduced liability totaled $225.3 million and amounted to a 23-percent reduction in Federal income taxes for those taking advantage of the provision, compared with the amount that they would have owed without income averaging. A large share of the total tax reduction was realized by farmers with adjusted gross income over $1 million. These farmers reduced their liability by an average of $264,000, for a total of $82.6 million.

While more recent data are not available, since farm income has trended higher in recent years the income averaging provision is likely to be of equal or greater benefit to farmers with substantial income growth. While a reduction in the number and level of marginal tax rates would reduce the savings under a new system, some farmers would still face higher tax rates due to income variability if the income averaging provision is eliminated.

Domestic Production Activities Deduction

One of the most important business changes in the American Jobs Creation Act of 2004 was the replacement of the foreign sales corporation/extraterritorial income provisions, which had allowed U.S. exporters to exclude a portion of their foreign sales income from taxation, with a new deduction for U.S. manufacturers, which includes farmers. The foreign sales corporation provision had been declared a prohibited export subsidy by the World Trade Organization, and its replacement was required to avoid retaliatory tariffs.

A domestic production activity includes an activity that involves the lease, rental, license, sale, exchange, or other disposition of tangible personal property that was manufactured, produced, grown, or extracted in whole or in significant part within the United States. It is not limited to exported goods.[16] Thus, while very few farm households directly benefited from the export provision, according to IRS tax data about 7 percent of farm households directly benefit from the new deduction. The deduction is limited to the lesser of 9 percent of adjusted gross income or domestic production activities income or 50 percent of wages paid to produce such income. While the wages-paid limitation reduces the deduction for many smaller farms that hire little or no labor, farm sole proprietors deducted nearly $1.25 billion in 2010. The average deduction for eligible farm households was $8,926. Among farms, commercial farm households are the primary beneficiaries since they are more likely to report positive farm income and wages paid to hired labor. Reducing or eliminating this deduction would result in a significant increase in taxable income for the beneficiaries of this deduction.

Self-Employed Health Insurance Deduction

The self-employed health insurance deduction was created in 1988 to give small business owners, including many farmers, tax benefits similar to those of employees who receive employer-deductible health insurance. This deduction is especially important for self-employed individuals who must purchase health insurance on their own.

Since 2003, farmers and other self-employed taxpayers have been allowed to deduct 100 percent of the cost of providing health insurance for themselves and their families as long as they are not eligible for any employer-sponsored plan. The self-employed health insurance deduction is limited to the amount of the taxpayer's income from self-employment. This limitation eliminates the deduction for farmers with net farm losses and no other self-employment income.

While IRS tax data indicate that only about 2.6 percent of all taxpayers utilize the self-employed health insurance deduction, about one out of seven farmers use the deduction in any given year. In 2010, these farmers deducted an average of $6,173 for a total of $1.684 billion in health insurance premiums. Over 50 percent of farm households obtain their insurance through off-farm employment of the operator or spouse, which helps account for the low number of farmers claiming the deduction. Many other farmers are over age 65 and are covered by Medicare or other Government programs (Jones et al., 2009).

Intermediate and commercial farmers are more likely than rural residence farmers to use the deduction. Only about 8 percent of rural residence farmers claim the deduction, primarily because greater proportions of these households receive health insurance from a nonfarm job or do not qualify for the deduction due to reporting a farm loss. The self-employed health insurance deduction allows farmers to save a portion of their premiums equal to their marginal tax rate, helping make health insurance more affordable and making the tax treatment more comparable to employer-sponsored plans.

TAXATION OF RURAL HOUSEHOLDS
UNDER PROPOSED REFORM

Tax reform would affect rural nonfarm households differently than farm and urban households. Rural nonfarm households have lower incomes, are older, and have higher poverty rates than urban households. In 2008, the average rural taxpayer reported an adjusted gross income (AGI) of $43,616, compared with $60,841 for the average urban taxpayer (Durst and Farrigan, 2011). Given their lower income, rural nonfarm households are less likely to benefit from tax deductions, exemptions, exclusions, or deferrals because they either lack eligible expenses to exceed the standard deduction or otherwise do not qualify for the tax benefits.[17] For example, some of the most widely used deductions—the deduction for mortgage interest and real estate taxes—are related to the value of property and real property tax rates, which are generally lower in rural areas (average annual rural real property taxes in 2009 were $1,639 for rural homeowners versus $3,393 for nonrural).[18] However, rural households are more likely to own homes and pay property taxes than urban households (table 5).

The age distribution of rural America also affects the impact of tax reform. Approximately 16.4 percent of the rural population is over the age of 65 (12.9 percent of the urban population is over the age of 65) (2012 Current Population Survey), and older adults generally have lower incomes, particularly from earned income, due to lower rates of labor force participation. Older adults also are less likely to use the tax system to receive tax benefits targeted to wage earners and families with children. Therefore, they are less likely to be required to file a tax return or to apply for a refundable credit.[19]

Because rural households are less likely to benefit from itemized deductions compared to urban households, proposals to eliminate deductions will have less effect on their well-being. On the other hand, rural nonfarm households are more likely than others to benefit from tax credits, particularly the refundable credits such as the Earned Income Tax Credit and the Child Tax Credit. The NCFRR co-chairs' report proposes to keep the current EITC and CTC intact; however, other reform plans seek to consolidate credits along the lines of work and family (appendix table A1). How rural nonfarm residents will fare under tax reform will depend in large part on how the credit system is changed.

Rural Homeowners Are Less Likely to Benefit from the Mortgage Interest Deduction

Itemized deductions are allowed for certain medical expenses, State and local taxes paid, mortgage interest paid, investment interest, charitable contributions, and a variety of miscellaneous expenses (see table 1).

The mortgage interest deduction is one of the largest tax expenditures in the Federal income tax system, and it is the largest Federal tax benefit for owner-occupied housing. This deduction allows taxpayers who own a home, have a mortgage, and itemize on their tax returns to deduct interest paid on up to $1.1 million of home mortgage debt.[20] The mortgage interest deduction primarily benefits homeowners in the top fifth of the income distribution (defined as household income of at least $98,000) because they are the taxpayers who are most likely to itemize. Thus, eliminating or scaling back the mortgage interest deduction would have a larger negative impact on high-income homeowners than on low- to middle-income homeowners.

Table 5. Homeowners with a mortgage by income group, share by residence, 2009

	Housing and mortgage statistics					
	Household income quintile					
Rural[a]	$0-$19,299	$19,300-36,465	$36,466-59,999	$60,000-97,999	$98,000 and above	All income groups
Own (%)	62	72.8	82.1	89.7	95.0	62.1
Mortgage (%)	14.7	27.8	46.0	58.7	64.6	30.8
% population	6	5	5	4	3	22
Mortgage value ($)[b]	83,799	79,657	91,859	113,979	180,483	112,464
Urban						
Own (%)	43.5	55.6	66.2	78.2	90.1	59.5
Mortgage (%)	15.6	26.5	42.4	58.7	72.0	38.8
% population	14	15	15	15	17	78
Mortgage value ($)[b]	119,905	124,536	140,754	167,274	260,771	187,244

Notes: *Own* is the percentage who own their residence; *Mortgage* is the percentage who have a mortgage on their owned residence; *% population* is the percentage of the U.S. population.

[a] Rural is defined as living outside of a Metropolitan Statistical Area.

[b] Mean value of original mortgage or mortgages.

Source: Authors' calculations using data from the American Housing Survey, 2009.

Toder et al. (2010) estimated that eliminating the mortgage interest deduction without replacing it with another tax preference would raise taxes, while reducing the after-tax income of all taxpayers by less than 1 percent, on average. In fact, if the tax expenditures for the mortgage interest deduction and property tax were eliminated, the after-tax income of the lowest quintile in the income distribution would be essentially unchanged.

However, these effects would vary greatly across income groups: 1 to 20 percent of taxpayers in the bottom to middle income quintiles would likely experience some increase in tax liability, compared to about 70 percent in the top income quintile.

The latter group is more likely to own homes, to itemize deductions, and to face higher marginal tax rates that tend to make deductions more valuable to them than to lower income taxpayers.

Various mortgage interest deduction reform options have been considered. Under the proposal by the co-chairs of the NCFRR, the mortgage interest deduction would be eliminated and replaced with a nonrefundable mortgage interest credit that would be available to both itemizers and non-itemizers. The Debt Reduction Task Force also proposed to eliminate the mortgage interest deduction, but replace it with a refundable credit, which would benefit taxpayers with mortgages who do not itemize or who do not have a tax liability—generally, taxpayers in the bottom three income quintiles.

On the other hand, taxpayers in the fourth quintile would gain the most from a nonrefundable (NCFRR) credit because they are more likely to have a positive tax liability to be offset with the credit. With either a refundable or a nonrefundable credit, those in the top quintile would likely experience a significant increase in the amount of income subject to tax and, depending upon the tax rate structure, could face higher taxes.

In general, based on their incomes, less than a third of rural households itemize their deductions. Urban taxpayers are more likely to benefit from the mortgage interest deduction and are more likely to face reductions to after-tax income if the mortgage interest deduction is eliminated; in fact, only 3 percent of the population resides in a rural area and has income that puts them in the top fifth of the income distribution (table 5).

The average mortgage value (including up to four mortgages) in 2009 was $112,464 for rural homeowners and $187,244 for urban homeowners.

On average, taxpayers in urban areas have higher incomes than their rural counterparts, and though they have lower rates of home ownership (table 5), they are more likely to have a mortgage, especially the urban residents in the top quintile of the income distribution.

Further, high-income rural homeowners are less likely than high-income urban homeowners to have a mortgage, and their mortgages are of lower value.

Thus, rural homeowners, especially in the lower three quintiles of the income distribution, currently receive little or no benefit from the mortgage interest deduction and may even benefit by replacing it with a refundable credit for mortgage interest.

Low-Income Rural Families Rely Heavily on Refundable Tax Credits

The major tax reform proposals each offer plans to create credits in lieu of deductions or to restructure the current credits. Although low-income families generally do not benefit from itemized deductions, they are primary beneficiaries of refundable tax credits, and how the system of credits is changed could have a substantial impact on their after-tax income. A tax credit, whether refundable or not, is applied after an individual's tax is computed.

Tax credits are an alternative to direct spending programs to accomplish specific policy objectives, and they have increasingly been used as a means to provide income support to low-income workers and families with children. Since 1980, the total cost of all tax expenditures or preferences has increased by over 250 percent and currently exceeds $1 trillion a year (The White House, 2010). Two of the most significant tax credits—the earned income tax credit (EITC) and child tax credit (CTC), which are refundable—accounted for $116 billion in tax expenditures in 2011 (table 1). In fact, the EITC has increasingly become one of the largest sources of cash assistance for low-income families. The refundable CTC also provides a significant amount of support. These two credits have significantly reduced the share of taxpayers who owe Federal income tax. For many low-income families, tax credit refunds represent a large share of their disposable income.

Both the EITC and CTC encourage work and help families with children meet basic needs. Since the EITC and CTC phase in with earnings, they encourage labor force participation among low-income single parents, to whom the tax credits are most valuable. While a phaseout of the EITC could arguably discourage a current recipient from working, research suggests that, overall, the EITC encourages work among recipient households.[21] A growing number of families (25.7 million in 2009) receive these benefits (fig. 3). In 2010, these two refundable tax credits represented nearly 15 percent of income for low-income families and approximately 25 percent of income for low-income families with children.[22]

Rural households have historically had lower incomes and higher poverty rates than urban households. Given the income differential and the prevalence of low-wage jobs, it is not surprising that rural taxpayers benefit disproportionately from tax programs targeting low-income workers, especially the EITC.

In 2008, 21.6 percent of rural taxpayers received EITC benefits, compared with 16.9 percent of urban taxpayers. The share of rural taxpayers who received the refundable portion of the child tax credit was also slightly higher, at 13.9 percent versus 12.6 percent for urban taxpayers. The earned income and child tax credits provided a total benefit of $20.6 billion to rural taxpayers in 2008. Overall, one out of every three rural taxpayers received benefits from the EITC or the CTC.

The refundable portion of the EITC and the CTC provides a significant boost ($13.7 billion in 2008) in income to rural taxpayers (table 6). For rural taxpayers with AGI under $10,000, these refundable credits were nearly one-third of AGI and averaged $1,276 in 2008. For those with income between $10,000 and $20,000, these refundable credits were nearly one-fourth of AGI and were $3,474, on average. Overall, EITC and CTC refunded tax credits provided a 13-percent increase in income to rural taxpayers receiving one or both of the credits in 2008.

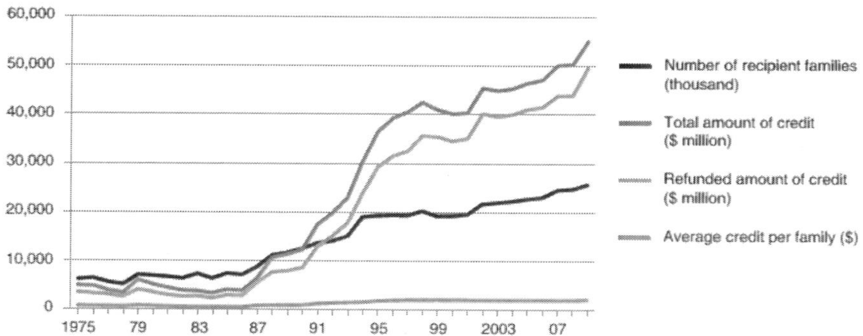

Source: USDA, Economic Research Service using data from the Internal Revenue Service.

Figure 3. Number of EITC recipient families, total amount of credit, and refunded amount of total (2009 dollars), 1975-2009.

Refundable tax credits, especially the EITC, have lifted a significant number of households above the poverty line. While the official measure of poverty does not include the EITC as a form of income, the Census Bureau publishes information on poverty under various alternative definitions. Comparing the poverty rate under the definition of income that includes various support programs and the EITC with the official poverty estimates for 2008 suggests a reduction in the rural poverty rate from 15.1 percent to 11.1 percent. The EITC alone was responsible for a reduction of 1.7 percentage points in the rural poverty rate. This suggests that in 2006 the EITC lifted an estimated 800,000 rural residents above the poverty line. Given expansions in the EITC that have occurred since 2006 as well as the expanded refundability of the child tax credit, the current impact on rural poverty of these tax-based policies is likely to be even greater.

Table 6. Refundable credits and adjusted gross income for rural taxpayers by level of adjusted gross income, 2008

	Rural taxpayers	Refundable earned income and child tax credits	Adjusted gross income	Credits as share of adjusted gross income
Adjusted gross income	*Thousand*	*$ Million*	*$ Million*	*Percent*
Under $10,000	5,148	2,026	6,442	31
$10,000 to $20,000	4,756	6,025	25,620	24
$20,001 to $25,000	1,965	2,383	16,148	15
$25,001 to $50,000	6,278	2,968	45,730	6
$50,001 to $100,000	5,352	273	12,472	2
Over $100,000	1,895	2	220	1
All	25,395	13,680	106,633	13

Source: USDA, Economic Research Service, based on special tabulations from 2008 Internal Revenue Service tax data.

The value of these credits suggests that their elimination or reduction would have a significant effect on low-income families, and rural families in particular, unless new programs were created to provide cash assistance. Most tax reform proposals would not eliminate these credits, but would consolidate them into new family and worker credits. The various options under consideration would reduce the number of credits and deductions and standardize eligibility rules. While it is suggested that this would eliminate much of the complexity, computational burden, taxpayer confusion, and difficulties with enforcement that are commonly cited by critics of the tax system, the changes could have a significant impact on the after-tax income of some rural households.

CONCLUSION

The primary goals of tax reform are to simplify the tax system, making it easier to comply with, and to reduce economic distortions induced by the system while preserving its progressive nature. While reform may improve societal welfare, the current tax system contains features that provide substantial benefit to farm businesses, and reform could reduce the after-tax income of many farm households. In particular, reducing or eliminating deductions for capital purchases and raising capital gains taxes could increase the farmers' tax base and raise the tax rate paid on a significant portion of their income. These effects will vary by farm size and type. Offsetting these effects, though, is the proposed reform of the marginal tax rate structure. A reduced number of brackets and lower rates will mitigate the effect of a potentially larger tax base for U.S. farm households.

Nonfarm rural households also have a major stake in tax reform. On average, rural households have lower incomes than the average U.S. household and receive significant benefits from the tax system's credits. Any reform that reduces the value of refundable credits, especially the Earned Income Tax Credit and Child Tax Credit, is likely to reduce the well-being of rural households. On the other hand, rural households are less likely to benefit from deductions and other adjustments to gross income. Therefore, eliminating or limiting these deductions will not have a large effect on most rural households. As with farmers, the net effect on Federal income tax liability and after-tax income will depend upon the specific details of tax base broadening and the restructuring of tax rates.

REFERENCES

Bipartisan Policy Center. 2010. Restoring America's Future: Reviving the Economy, Cutting Spending and Debt, and Creating a Simple, Pro-Growth Tax System. Washington, DC. Nov.

Brill, A., and A. Viard. 2011. "The Benefits and Limitation of Income Tax Reform," Tax Policy Outlook, no. 2. American Enterprise Institute for Public Policy. Sept.

Dickert, S., S. Houser, and J.K. Scholz. 1995. "The earned income tax credit and transfer programs: a study of labor market and program participation," Tax Policy and the Economy, vol. 9. J. Poterba (ed.), MIT Press, Cambridge, MA.

Durst, Ron, and Tracey Farrigan. 2011. Federal Tax Policies and Low-Income Rural Households, EIB-76, U.S. Department of Agriculture, Economic Research Service, May.

Durst, R. and J. Monke. "Effects of Federal Tax Policy on Agriculture." Food and Rural Economics Division, Economic Research Service, U.S. Department of Agriculture, Agricultural Economic Report No. 800. Washington, DC, April 2001.

Eissa, N. and H. Williamson Hoynes. 2004. "Taxes and the labor market participation of married couples: the earned income tax credit" Journal of Publics Economics 88:1931-1958.

Goode, R. 1976, Individual Income Taxation, The Brookings Institution, Washington, DC.

Government Accountability Office. 2011. "TAX GAP: Complexity and Taxpayer Compliance" Report GAO-11-747T, Tuesday, June 28.

Government Accountability Office. 2007. "Tax Administration: 2007 Filing Season Continues Trend of Improvement, but Opportunities to Reduce Costs and Increase the Tax Compliance Should be Evaluated," Report GAO-08-38, Nov.

Government Accountability Office. 2003. "PAID TAX PREPARERS: Most Taxpayers Believe They Benefit, but Some Are Poorly Served," Report GAO-03-610T, April 1.

Hausman, J. 1981. "Labor Supply" in How Taxes Affect Economic Behavior, H. Aaron and J. Pechman (eds.), pp. 27-72, Brookings Institution, Washington, DC.

Jones, Carol, Timothy Park, Mary Ahearn, Ashok K. Mishra, and Jayachandran Variyam. 2009. Health Status and Health Care Access of Farm and Rural Populations. EIB-57, U.S. Department of Agriculture, Economic Research Service, Aug.

Kaiser Family Foundation and the Health Research and Educational Trust. 2011. Employer Health Benefits: 2011 Annual Survey, Menlo Park, CA.

MaCurdy, T., D. Green, and H. Paarsch. 1990 . "Assessing empirical approaches for analyzing taxes and labour supply," Journal of Human Resources 25: 415-490.

Meyer, B., and D. Rosenbaum. 2001. "Welfare, the earned income tax credit, and the labor supply of single mothers," Quarterly Journal of Economics 116 (3) (August).

Mishra, Ashok K., Hisham S. El-Osta, Mitchell J. Morehart, James D. Johnson, and Jeffrey W. Hopkins. 2002. Income, Wealth, and the Economic Well-Being of Farm Households. AER-812, July.

National Commission on Fiscal Responsibility and Reform. 2010. Moment of Truth: Report of the National Commission on Fiscal Responsibility and Reform. Dec.

Office of Management and Budget. 2012. The Fiscal Year 2013 Budget of the United States Government: Analytical Perspectives: http://www. whitehouse.gov/sites/default/files/omb/budget/fy2013/assets/spec.pdf

Piketty, T, and E. Saez. 2007. "How Progressive is the U.S. Federal Tax System? A Historical and International Perspective," Journal of Economic Perspectives 21 (1) Winter: 3-24.

President's Economic Recovery Advisory Board. 2010. The Report on Tax Reform Options: Simplification, Compliance, and Corporate Taxation. Aug.

Toder, E., M. Turner, K. Lim, and L. Getsinger. 2010. Reforming the Mortgage Interest Deduction. Urban Institute and Brookings Institution Tax Policy Center.

Triest, Robert K. 1990. "The Effect of Income Taxation on Labor Supply in the United States," The Journal of Human Resources, Vol. 25, No. 3.

U.S. Congress. Congressional Budget Office. 2011. The Budget and Economic Outlook: Fiscal Years 2011 to 2021, Jan.

Appendix Table A1. Major reform proposal provisions

	Current law	NCFRR	PERAB	BPC
Tax rates for individuals				
Ordinary income	10, 15, 25, 28, 33, 35, 39.6 %	Three brackets with a target of 12, 22, 29%	N.A.	Two brackets: 15, 27%
Capital gains and dividends	0, 15, 18.8, 20, 23.8%	Tax at ordinary rates	Tax at ordinary rates with an exclusion for 50% of gains	Tax at ordinary rates (not greater than 27%), with an exclusion for fi rst $1,000 of gain or loss
Standard deduction	$6,100 single $12,200 married	No change	Increase value	Eliminate
Itemized deductions	Limits on itemized deductions for those with adjusted gross income over $250,000 ($300,000 joint return)	Eliminate	Reduce the value of itemizing by limiting cost of expenses (<100%)	Eliminate and replace many of the deductions with a tax credit; allow deductions in excess of 5% of AGI
Credits	Mix of refundable and non-refundable credits	Maintain current law EITC and Child Tax Credit; create non-refundable credits for mortgage interest, charitable	Consolidate common credits along the themes of work and family; simplify the eligibility rules	Create a refundable per-child tax credit of $1,600; create a 21.3% refundable earnings credit;

Appendix Table A1. (Continued)

	Current law	NCFRR	PERAB	BPC
		giving, and retirement savings		15% refundable credits for charitable giving and mortgage interest; 15% credits for education and retirement savings; AGI phase-outs for some credits
National sales tax	None	N.A.	N.A.	6.5% phased in over 2 years

N.A. = not applicable.

Sources: National Commission on Fiscal Responsibility and Reform (NCFRR), December 2010, "Moment of Truth"; President's Economic Recovery Advisory Board (PERAB), August 2010, "The Report on Tax Reform Options: Simplifi cation, Compliance and Corporate Taxation"; Bipartisan Policy Center (BPC), November 2010, "Restoring American's Future: Reviving the Economy, Cutting Spending and Debt, and Creating a Simple, Pro-growth Tax System."

Appendix Table A2. Farm Typology

Farm Types	
Small family farms (gross sales less than $250,000)	Large-scale family farms (gross sales of $250,000 or more)
Rural-residence family farms:	Commercial family farms:
Retirement farms. Small farms whose operators report they are retired.	Large family farms. Gross sales between $250,000 and $499,999.
Residential/lifestyle farms. Small farms whose operators report a major occupation other than farming.	Very large family farms. Gross sales of $500,000 or more
	Nonfamily farms
Intermediate family farms:	Any farm not classifi ed as a family farm, that is, any farm for which the majority of the farm business is not owned by individuals related by blood, marriage, or adoption.
Farming-occupation farms. Small family farms whose operators report farming as their major occupation.	
• Low-sales farms. Gross sales less than $100,000. • High-sales farms. Gross sales between $100,000 and $249,999.	

End Notes

[1] Rural is defined as nonmetropolitan, which is any area that is not part of a Metropolitan Statistical Area (MSA).

[2] As provided by its bylaws, the Commission was required to vote on the approval of a final report. On Dec. 3, 2010, a vote was held on a plan forwarded by the panel's 2 chairs, Alan Simpson and Erskine Bowles; however, it fell short of the supermajority of 14 needed to send a proposal to Congress. This analysis examines the proposals of the Commission's co-chairs (National Commission on Fiscal Responsibility and Reform, 2010).

[3] Tax expenditures are sometimes known as "tax preferences," evoking an image that the benefits accrue to a small group or a narrowly defined activity. However, in some cases, an individual tax expenditure benefits a large proportion of taxpayers. The exclusion from income allowed for the employer contribution toward health insurance is one example.

[4] The effect of taxes on labor supply varies by demographic; the labor supply of prime-age (ages 25-54) men is estimated to be very insensitive to taxes (Hausman, 1981; MaCurdy et al., 1990), while the labor supply of women, particularly married women and women with children, is estimated to be more sensitive (Hausman. 1981; Dickert et al., 1995).

[5] Eissa and Williamson-Hoynes (2004) find that married women in the phaseout range of the EITC are less likely to work.

[6] Created by Executive Order 13531.

[7] A nonrefundable credit is applied up to only the amount of a taxpayer's tax liability. If the value of a nonrefundable credit is more than the amount of tax, the taxpayer's tax liability is reduced to zero. In contrast, a refundable credit may entitle the individual to receive a refund for the amount in excess of tax liability.

[8] The current maximum rate is 39.6 percent.

[9] Senator Pete Domenici and Dr. Alice Rivlin, co-chairs.

[10] Corporate taxes are levied on the net income of the corporation; individual taxes are based on the adjusted gross income of the individual.

[11] 2008 Internal Revenue Service (IRS) data indicate that as many as 64 percent of corporate farms have business receipts of less than $250,000 (IRS, SOI Tax Stats, Table 5: Returns of Active Corporations 2008).

[12] [C]attle and horses, regardless of age, held by the taxpayer for draft, breeding, dairy, or sporting purposes, and held by him for 24 months or more from the date of acquisition, and (B) other livestock, regardless of age, held by the taxpayer for draft, breeding, dairy, or sporting purposes, and held by him for 12 months or more from the date of acquisition. Such term does not include poultry (IRC Section 1231(b)(3)).

[13] Internal Revenue Service, Statistics of Income, Special Tabulations for *Farm Proprietorships, 2010.*

[14] See appendix table A2 for typologies of farms.

[15] The amount is reduced (but not below zero) by the amount by which the investment exceeds $2,000,000.

[16] Domestic production activities income is the excess of domestic production gross receipts for the tax year minus the sum of the cost of goods sold and other expenses, losses, or deductions (other than the domestic production activities deduction) allocable to such receipts (IRC Section 199).

[17] Standard deduction for married couples filing jointly in 2011 was $11,900.

[18] Authors' calculations from the 2009 American Housing Survey, Department of Commerce, Bureau of the Census.

[19] Social Security benefits are not taxed if a taxpayer's modified adjusted gross income plus one-half of their Social Security benefits are below a certain amount ($32,000 for married couples filing jointly in 2011); however, if a beneficiary's "provisional" income exceeds that amount, part of the Social Security benefit may be taxed.

[20] The provision allows for $1 million for mortgage debt plus $100,000 of home equity debt.

[21] For example, while Eissa and Williamson-Hoynes (2004) find evidence that married women reduced their labor force participation in response to an expansion of the EITC, others such as a Meyer and Rosenbaum (2001) find that single mothers work more in response to the EITC.

[22] Estimates based on 2011 Current Population Survey, tax model data for 2010.

INDEX